HE RESTORES MY SOUL

Leatrice Nash

This book may contain quotations from the Bible. The specific translations used are as follows:

New King James Version (NKJV)
Scripture taken from the New King James Version®. Copyright © 1982 by Thomas Nelson. Used by permission. All rights reserved.

New International Version (NIV)
Scripture taken from the Holy Bible, New International Version®, NIV®. Copyright © 1973, 1978, 1984, 2011 by Biblica, Inc.® Used by permission. All rights reserved worldwide.

King James Version (KJV)
Scripture taken from the King James Version. Public Domain.

Contemporary English Version (CEV)
Scripture taken from the Contemporary English Version (CEV). Copyright © 1995 by the American Bible Society. Used by permission. All rights reserved.

Amplified Bible (AMP)
Scripture quotations taken from the Amplified® Bible (AMP), Copyright © 2015 by The Lockman Foundation. Used by permission. www.lockman.org

The Message (MSG)
Scripture taken from The Message. Copyright © 1993, 2002, 2018 by Eugene H. Peterson. Used by permission of NavPress. All rights reserved. Represented by Tyndale House Publishers, Inc.

Cover Design:
Apostle Latonia Moore

Printed in United States of America.

October 2024

TABLE OF CONTENT

DEDICATION

This book is dedicated to my mentor, my teacher and my mother in the faith, Apostle Latonia Moore. The one who saw a spark and fanned it until it became a flame.

This book is the brainchild of a conversation that I had with Apostle Moore. "Now that you have the souls, what are you going to do with them"? This question ignited the flame and prompted a 21-day teaching on He Restores My Soul. Many lives were impacted.

To my mother, Wanda Alexander. Thank you for not allowing me to give up. Even when life was cruel, you were always my "safe place". I love you mommy.

Ms. Nash

Apostle Latonia Moore

Wanda Alexander

CHAPTER 01

THE OIL PRESS

Evangelist Leatrice Nash

> ❝
>
> *Father if you are willing remove this cup from me: Nevertheless, not my will but thine be done.*
> **-Luke 22:42**
>
> ❞

Have you ever felt like life was being pressed out of you? Have you ever wanted to give up? Have you ever been in a battle between your will and the will of the Father? If you answered yes to any of these questions, you have likely found yourself at the "Oil Press." The "Oil Press" is the place of crushing—it's the place where you lay down your will and choose the will of the Father, despite how it crushes your flesh. One of the most challenging and frightening things I had to learn was how to give God a "yes" even in a low and frightening place. Often the Father will require you to accomplish something that seems so far out of your reach and you fail to move forward because you were looking at it through the lens of fear. Not only does the "Oil Press" require obedience but it also requires dependency on the power of the Holy Spirit that is at work on the inside of you.

In Luke 22:42 we see the human side of Jesus as He approached the fulfillment of His purpose to bear the sins of the world. Jesus' only purpose was to fulfill the will of the Father, even to the point of death. In His human state, Jesus was afraid of the suffering He was about to endure. We see this in Mark 14:4 where Jesus said to the disciples, "My soul is exceedingly sorrowful unto death." While falling to the ground in desperation and with bloody sweat rolling from His face, Jesus offered up a cry to the Father, asking for the time of suffering to be removed from Him, but nevertheless, thy will be done. This act was a demonstration of Christ's obedience to the will of the Father. In John 4:34, Jesus said to them, "My food is to do the will of him who sent me and to accomplish his work (ESV).

Holy Spirit helps us in our weaknesses and teaches us how to pray according to the will of God. Even in the "Oil Press," Holy Spirit is present strengthening us and giving us the power to do what pleases God. Jesus endured the cross, disregarded the shame, and now is seated at the right hand of the throne of God (Hebrews 12:2).

Beloved, meditate on this, there is glory after the suffering. When you go through various trials, take into consideration how Jesus endured such hatred, humiliation, and hostility, so that you and I may have a new life in Christ. Consider Romans 5: 3-5, which says we glory in our sufferings, because suffering produces perseverance, perseverance produces character and character produces hope. The "Oil Press" is not designed to hurt you but designed to mature you that Christ may be formed in you.

Prayer:

Father, according to Your word You are always with me. Make Your presence known to me even more that I may overcome every obstacle sent to impede my spiritual development.

Thank You Heavenly Father that when I go through the fire, You promise to be with me. When I go through the flood, the waters will not overtake me. Teach me how to trust You, even in the difficult seasons and give me unyielding faith in Your word that I may be steadfast through every trial.

ABOUT THE VISIONARY

Evangelist Leatrice Nash is the co-founder of Palisade Where Hope Is Renewed, a non-profit organization dedicated to providing supportive services to at-risk youth in the Central Texas area. She is also the founder and host of Hope Renewed Global, a marketplace ministry that empowers women daily to become their best selves through prayer, biblical principles, and accountability.

In October 2022, Evangelist Nash launched the 21 Day Prayer Challenge, a prayer line where both men and women gather to be refreshed through prayer and the Word of God. This initiative has significantly impacted many lives.

Evangelist Nash's other evangelistic efforts include the Woman Arise Women's Conference, an event that attracts women from around the world and has propelled many into their God-given assignments. As a spiritual midwife and mentor, she leverages her experiences to guide women in walking in their purpose and fulfilling God's call on their lives.

As a single parent, Evangelist Nash persevered through challenges to earn a Master's Degree from Stephen F. Austin State University in 2016 and is currently pursuing a Doctoral Degree in Strategic Leadership from Liberty University.

She is a dedicated member of Victorious Life Christian Center in San Antonio, Texas, where she serves under the apostolic leadership of Apostle Latonia Moore. Despite her professional and academic accomplishments, Evangelist Nash finds her most rewarding roles in being a mother, grandmother, and minister of the Gospel of Jesus Christ.

CHAPTER 02

WHEN HIS WORD IS ALL YOU HAVE

DeAndrea (Dee) Williams

> 66
>
> *And Abraham called the name of that place Jehovah-jireh: as it is said to this day, In the mount of the LORD it shall be seen.*
> **-Genesis 22:14 (KJV)**
>
> 99

Many of us can recall times when life becomes challenging, and it feels like there's no way out of a difficult situation. The future seems uncertain, and the outcome doesn't appear to be in your favor. You know those moments when hope feels distant and a positive outcome unlikely. These are the times beyond the phrase "Life be life'n" -when everything spirals out of YOUR control, and it feels like the walls are closing in. You might be facing job loss, months—yes months—behind on mortgage and car payments, with other mounting bills. To top it off, the kids are "acting a fool," as my grandmother would say. And to add to the unending list, your parents are aging, and their health is not the best.

There are times when God guides you to take a certain action, yet the path forward seems unclear.

Perhaps it's about allowing a child to grow into their own person and relinquishing control, fully trusting them to God's care. These practical steps might seem effortless for others, but for you, the fear and uncertainty of the outcome can feel paralyzing.

These moments come to us all. They may not align exactly with what I've mentioned, but at some point in your relationship with Christ, you will face fear, uncertainty, and doubt. These are the times I have learned to lean into God's word the most. One of my favorite passages, which I refer to as my "grounding" scripture, is Genesis 22. In this chapter, God tests Abraham by instructing him to take his son Isaac—his only, beloved, and promised son—to Moriah and offer him as a burnt offering. The scriptures tell us that Abraham was obedient.

Because my imagination can run wild and the human side of me always seeks understanding, I can imagine that Abraham had some questions. I imagine Abraham's thoughts might have been, "Are you sure, God? My son Isaac? My promised son?" I can further imagine him thinking, "God, you told me I would be the father of many nations, and now you want me to sacrifice my promised child? Lord, you know how hard it was for Sarah and me to have this one, and now you want ME to kill him?" However, the scripture does not detail this; it merely recounts Abraham's act of obedience and his trust in God's word. Abraham trusted God and in response, God provided a sacrifice in place of his son (Genesis 22:13). This act occurred because Abraham had complete faith in God. We see in the following scripture that Abraham proclaimed "Jehovah Jireh," meaning "The Lord will provide" (Genesis 22:14).

Today, the things God asks of us are minor compared to what was asked of Abraham. God gives us the choice to trust His word.

We just need to have faith and believe, regardless of whether we know the outcome. During life's uncertainties and testing times, which are "for our good" and to make us stronger in Him, are a part of His plan for us. We must hold on to His word and trust that He will provide ALL of our needs.

Prayer:

Heavenly Father, I come to You today humbly and with an open heart, asking that You continuously grow my faith in You. Lord, please help me to recognize Your voice without doubt or uncertainty, so that I may move forward on Your word without hesitation or question. Let me learn and retain the scriptures, so that in times of uncertainty, I can draw strength from Your promises and Your will for my life. In Jesus' name, Amen.

ABOUT THE AUTHOR

DeAndrea Williams, a Louisiana native now residing in the Pacific Northwest near Seattle, WA, brings a diverse perspective from her experiences living between these two states. Known as Dee, she is an active community supporter and church member, dedicating her time to volunteering and working with young mothers.

Professionally, Dee serves as a Project Manager and Trauma-Informed Care Facilitator for a non-profit organization, where she integrates NEAR (Neurodevelopment, Epigenetics, Adverse Childhood Experiences, and Resilience) Sciences with spirituality and biblical principles.

Dee is married to her husband, Darren, for 18 years, and is a devoted mother to three sons and a proud "Mimi" to three grandchildren.

CHAPTER 03

IT AIN'T WHAT IT LOOKS LIKE

Chauncy D. Craig

> **"** *"Therefore, if anyone is in Christ, he is a new creation; old things have passed away; behold, all things have become new."* [1]
> **--2 Corinthians 5:17 (NKJV)** **"**

Life experiences, mishaps, shortcomings, deficiencies, trauma, and other challenges inevitably shape our thoughts and identity. Unfortunately, the stigma of these less favorable aspects can linger even after we receive salvation. Why? They become the filter through which we measure ourselves or the mirror in which we see ourselves. Although these challenges are facts, they do not represent the truth! Therefore, pause, take a moment, and recognize that it ain't what it looks like.

---

[1] Unless otherwise noted, all biblical passages referenced are in the New King James Version (Nashville, TN: Thomas Nelson, 1982).

The scripture provides the truth: we are a new creation, and old things have passed away, including those past issues that seek to limit us and keep us bound to our former selves. Furthermore, verses 18-19 tell us about the reconciliation God offers us when we accept and embrace our new identity. If we can believe God's truth, we must understand that it ain't what it looks like. It ain't what it looks like in our memories, in the mirror, to our friends, or to those who witnessed our past struggles. It ain't what it looks like to the whispers of doubt from the enemy!

Beloved, it ain't what it looks like, feels like, tastes like, or sounds like. Why? Because God says, "Therefore, if anyone is in Christ, he is a new creation; old things have passed away; behold, all things have become new." According to the Bible dictionary, the Greek word for "new" -prosphatos- means "lately made."[2] So, when we or others try to remind us of our past, we can confidently declare that it was not us. We have been recently made new, and the old self has passed away. We have been restored, and our soul has been renewed.

It may sound unusual or even funny to some, and it might raise eyebrows, but it is the truth. You have been made new, reconciled with God, and restored to a relationship with Him. Forgive yourself, rise up, be restored, and walk in your newness, unshackled from your former life. God gladly restores our souls.

---

[2] James Strong, The New Strong's Complete Dictionary of Bible Words (Nashville, TN: Thomas Nelson Publishers, 1996), 177.

Prayer:

Dear Lord, Your Word tells me that You are the lifter of my head and that Your name is a strong tower, a place of safety to which we can run. Therefore, I come to You, seeking restoration and to assume my rightful position to be used for Your glory. You know everything about me, how I see myself, and all the limitations that hinder me. Yet, Your Word assures me that nothing is too hard for You. Please restore me, make me new, reconcile me to Yourself, and help me see myself as You see me. Remove yesterday's matters from my sight so I can confidently and intentionally recognize that I am indeed made new and that old things have passed away. Empower me to encourage others with this message, knowing that it ain't what it looks like, feels like, or tastes like. I thank You in advance and am determined to walk as if it is already done, with a restored soul, in Jesus' name. Amen!

ABOUT THE AUTHOR

Apostle Chauncy D. Craig hails from Florida and is the third of four children born to Calvin and Ann. He grew up in a loving but dysfunctional single-parent home, with his mother being a devout Christian. The challenges of his upbringing led to a period of violence and anger in his life, marked by frequent fights, school transfers, and several arrests.

Despite these early struggles, Apostle Craig has been married to Jacqueline for over 36 years, and together they have two sons. He served in the U.S. Army for over 21 years, retiring with the rank of E-8/MSG. Since October 1997, he has been deeply involved in God's redemptive work.

Apostle Craig holds a Master's Degree in Christian Leadership from Liberty University. He currently serves as the Apostle of Discipling Ministries Inc. in Radcliff, KY, an organization he founded in March 2010. His ministry focuses on discipleship, emphasizing the importance of making disciples of Christ rather than adhering to church doctrines, denominations, traditions, or human authority.

CHAPTER 04

ARE YOU WILLING?

Shequitta Arnold

> **❝** *Come now, let us reason together, saith the Lord: though your sins be as scarlet, they shall be as white as snow; though they be red like crimson, they shall be as wool. If ye be willing and obedient, ye shall eat the good of the land:*
> **-Isaiah 1:18-19 (KJV)** **❞**

Just like God offered forgiveness and cleansing to the people of Judah and Jerusalem, He is offering the same to us today. The book of Isaiah is a message of warning and hope. Matthew Henry's Concise commentary says, "Though we have often dipped into sin, by many backslidings; yet pardoning mercy will take out the stain." It does not matter how far we think we have fallen, or how bad it may seem, God will cleanse us of all our sins. The Bible says in 1 John 1:9 (NIV) that "If we confess our sins, He is faithful and just and will forgive our sins and purify us from all unrighteousness." However, God's forgiveness and cleansing was conditional based on their willingness to be obedient to God. The definition of willing according to dictionary.com, means cheerfully consenting or ready: a willing worker.

The word obedient means to comply with or be submissive to authority. We must willingly submit to God's authority and align our actions with His teachings. If we are not being obedient and trusting God, then we cannot expect God to release His blessings. The more we obey God and be obedient to His word, we become His friend.

John 15:14 (KJV) says, "Ye are my friends if ye do whatsoever I command you." It blows my mind to know that God is willing to be a friend to anyone willing to obey Him. I remember a time when I was disobedient and living in sin, I refused to obey the voice of God. He warned me so many times, but I continued to live a life of sin. He stepped back and allowed things to take place that would have cost me 30 years of my life. He gave me a choice to either turn my life around or to continue in sin. I was willing and obedient to follow God. I chose to live my life to the service of the Lord. By me doing so, God showed Himself mighty in my situation and today I am a free woman walking in God.

The more we obey God, we will develop a closer relationship with Him. When we are obedient to God, we will bear good fruit. When our will becomes God's will, then we will tap into the blessings of God. When we follow God's commands, we have the right to the benefits and blessings of God. Psalm 84:11(KJV) tells us "No good thing will He withhold from them that walk uprightly." It does not matter what we have done, there is Hope in God. If we are willing, God can and will restore us. He has given us a choice. It is up to us to make the decision to be willing and obedient so we can eat the good of the land. We have a right to the blessings and promises of God. What will you decide? Are you willing?

Prayer:

Dear Lord,

We come to You asking for forgiveness of all our sins. Though they be red like crimson, they shall be as white as snow. Lord, I submit my life to You, wash me whiter than snow. Expose my heart oh God. Remove everything that is not like You. I renounce those things that are not pleasing to You and I thank You for loving me enough to give me a choice. Lord, I choose You. Thank You, God for being my friend. Because I choose You, Lord, I shall eat the good of the land. You said in Your word in Psalm 84:11, "No good thing will You withhold from those who walk uprightly before You. God, I choose to walk upright today. God my desire is to be willing and obedient. I give You, my yes. I declare and decree that I will no longer allow my past or fear to hold me hostage. For You said in Isaiah 41:10 (KJV), "Fear not, for You are with me; be not dismayed, for You are my God; You will strengthen me, You will help me, You will uphold me with Your righteous right hand. Lord, thank You for restoring my soul. Amen!

ABOUT THE AUTHOR

Shequitta Arnold is a devoted wife, mother of five, and grandmother of four. She has previously served as President of SSLC and Parliamentarian for Skills USA within the Technical College System of Georgia. Currently, she is pursuing her Bachelor's Degree in Biblical Studies. In her leisure time, Shequitta enjoys reading, spending time at the beach, and fishing with her husband. She is passionate about her faith and is dedicated to encouraging others and offering hope through Christ.

CHAPTER 05

THE DRY BONES WILL LIVE!

Donna M. Lofton

> **❝** *So I prophesied as He commanded me, and breath came into them, and they lived, and stood up upon their feet, an exceeding great army.*
> **–Ezekiel 37:10 NKJV** **❞**

When was the last time you stopped to listen and obey what the Spirit of the Lord has been saying to you? I challenge you to sit with God in this moment. Look around and re-evaluate where you are in your life right now. Is this place where God has you, or is it a place you've created for yourself? Are you stuck here, refusing or feeling afraid to move?

Sometimes, we find ourselves in a place of isolation or despair, searching for restoration or facing situations that don't align with God's promises. In this season, if you desire to see a move of God, you must spend more time with Him— in His word, in prayer, and in fasting. God is calling you into a deeper relationship and connection with Him. He has been trying to reach you and those connected to you. Will you let Him in? Will you answer the call?

At times, we see only dry seasons and stagnation and may fear that God has forgotten about us. But He hasn't. God promised He will never leave us or forsake us. He is right there with you in this moment. Listen, God desires to move in your life, and He is waiting for you to be intentional—to stop, listen, and hear His word. Begin cultivating your relationship with the Father. Once you hear what He is saying and surrender to His word, action must follow.

In the vision of the Valley of Dry Bones in Ezekiel 37, God commanded Ezekiel to prophesy over the dry bones and then to prophesy over the breath of the bones. Through Ezekiel's obedience, an entire army arose. God is so good! It was through Ezekiel's obedience that he saw the move of God. This is what God wants from us: "to hear and obey," and then we will begin to see the salvation of the Lord.

God has already given us the authority to overcome all power of the enemy, according to Luke 10:19. We must decree and declare the promises God has made and trust that "no good thing will He withhold from us." He knows every need and everything we don't need. Trust Him. Trust that He will supply your needs according to His riches in glory. Restoration is happening. Life is being restored. Prophesy. Speak the words God has given you. Speak His promises and walk in obedience.

As you surrender and spend more time in prayer and in the word of God, you will come to a better understanding of the authority He has placed within you. Understanding contributes to our confidence, empowering you not only to speak but also to believe what you declare.

Again, I challenge you to incorporate this exercise into your devotional time. Set your intentions for greater things and reflect on every dry place in your life, whether it be remnants of past hurts, stagnation, or areas needing restoration and correction.

As you sit in this moment, take note of every situation that doesn't align with the word of God. Search out scriptures that apply to each situation and pray God's word over every matter you've noted.

Prayer:

Father, according to Your word, You have given me the authority to trample on the serpent's head. I speak to every dry place in my life and command it to LIVE. We call a ceasefire in this very moment; restoration is happening right now; life is being restored; dry bones, come to life. I decree and declare that every move of God be activated and function in the name of Jesus today. Restoration is here and it is yours!

ABOUT THE AUTHOR

Donna Lofton was born into a large family as the youngest of twelve children, affectionately referred to by her mother as "The Twelve Disciples." Raised in the southern part of South Georgia, Donna was groomed from an early age to become a minister of the gospel. She accepted Christ as her Lord and Savior at the age of nineteen.

Donna currently attends Victorious Life Christian Center. She is a proud mother to three handsome young men, a wonderful daughter-in-love, and a beautiful granddaughter. Her spiritual goal is to stay close to heaven, ensuring that chains and curses are broken from her bloodline. Inspired by her family and the Kingdom of God, Donna strives to be the best version of herself, recognizing that without spiritual action, she might hinder the generation she is ordained to reach.

Donna has been on her faith journey for over twenty years. Although it has not always been easy and there have been times she wanted to give up, she realized that she cannot live without God by her side. As she matures in the gospel, Donna learns that each day is a journey requiring a conscious decision about whom she will serve. She understands that this walk has many layers to shed, and by seeking and pressing towards the highest calling of God, she believes she will emerge as pure gold.

CHAPTER 06

LISTEN WITH CHILDLIKE WONDER

Leticia Botello

> **66** *"Now the Lord came and stood and called as at other times. 'Samuel! Samuel!' And Samuel answered, 'Speak, for Your servant hears.'"*
> **-1 Samuel 3:10 (NKJV)**
> **99**

How many times have you thought about a missed job opportunity, a relationship you thought would stand the test of time or other major life event and wondered why things hadn't worked out the way you planned? Have you tried to nudge things along in order to orchestrate an outcome that worked well for you? Have you ever asked God, "Why didn't You make this happen for me?" How many times have we asked those very questions but were not prepared to hear God's response?

Oftentimes we are so busy with our day to day lives, eager to check something else off our to-do list or scroll through social media that we are not focused on hearing God's voice. How many opportunities or blessings do you think you have missed by not being prepared to receive His word?

In this verse, Samuel was so focused on the natural, that it had not occurred to him that God could be speaking to him. Had it not been for Eli redirecting him, what might Samuel have missed?

Don't let the distractions of the world keep you from hearing His Word. Study the Word of God daily. Pray to grow a relationship with God and spend time meditating on Him. Be still in your private place and let Him know that you are ready to receive His word. Once Samuel understood the assignment, he could not wait to hear God's voice. Be like Samuel, so childlike in his eagerness to hear God's word, "Here I am, Lord. Your servant is ready!"

Our God is such a loving Father and He wants us to speak to him daily but like any parent, He also wants us to be ready to listen as well. Prepare yourself to listen with childlike wonder for God will share His plans with you in His time. Be patient. Be faithful. Be prepared to move when He instructs you to and be ready to reap the reward for your obedience.

Prayer:

Father God, I thank You for giving me ears to hear, a spirit with which to love, and wisdom to recognize that only through You, all things are possible. I humbly ask for Your help to overcome the distractions of the world so that I can be ready to hear Your instructions and to move when directed. Your servant is ready, please use me to grow your kingdom. In Jesus' name, Amen.

ABOUT THE AUTHOR

Leticia Botello works in higher education and has dedicated her career to helping people achieve their academic goals. She has spent almost twenty-five years encouraging people to see beyond their circumstances and to put their trust in God and to reclaim their strength. Not too long ago, Leticia was a lost soul but by the grace of God, was saved and she has now fully surrendered her life to honor Him and loves to share her testimony and her journey with others.

Like with anything of importance, Leticia works daily to live a life that glorifies God and even though she might fall short, she knows that God is a loving and forgiving Father and with just a mustard seed of faith, she can overcome any obstacle and even when things seem bleak, she reminders herself, "I can do all things, through Christ who strengthens me," (Philippians 4:13).

When Leticia is not studying God's good word and enjoying prayer time, she is busy running her faith inspired online shop, Thy Will Creations, which focuses on glorifying God and spreading his word to others. She can also be found singing loudly to worship music, tending to her garden and spending quality time with her adult son and the family dogs.

CHAPTER 07

YOU WERE MADE FOR THIS MOMENT

Apostle Dr. Karliss Kimbrough

> 66 *"Praise be to the Lord, the God of Israel, who has sent you today to meet me. May you be blessed for your good judgment and for keeping me from bloodshed this day and avenging myself with my own hands."*
> **-1 Samuel 25:32-33** 99

Have you ever found yourself in a situation at home similar to Abigail's? Like her, I had a husband whom I could never seem to please. Although his verbal abuse did not start off that way, the period of my life became incredibly challenging, and I often wondered how it all went so wrong. It's never easy to endure rudeness and unruly behavior from those we love. Their negative actions can leave you feeling embarrassed, frustrated, and depressed. Knowing that you'll be apologizing and accepting blame for their behavior can be overwhelming. If not careful, such behaviors can escalate to dangerous levels, potentially jeopardizing the entire household, marriage, professional life, and relationships with friends and family.

1 Samuel 25:2-42 describes Abigail's experience with her husband Nabal, who was rude, ill-tempered, and a drunkard. While the Bible does not specify whether Abigail faced mental or physical abuse, his contemptuous nature may have contributed to a difficult environment. Despite her struggles, Abigail's resilience and faithfulness shone through. Her commitment to God allowed her to influence those around her positively.

Abigail's simple yet profound prayer, "My Lord, let this blame be upon me and forgive the offenses," was instrumental in saving her family from destruction. By understanding the intricacies of her household, she ensured that disaster was averted. If you find it challenging to manage your home, life, and relationships while serving others, seek guidance from the Holy Spirit and be sincere in your prayers.

David said, "Praise be to God, who sent you today to meet me. May you be blessed for your good judgment." Abigail's brave and wise intervention provided David and his followers with the necessities they needed, quelling his anger and softening his heart. This act of courage was honored by God, and it demonstrates that even when life seems uncertain, God has a plan for you, filled with hope and a promising future (Jeremiah 29:11).

You were made for this moment, so don't let bitterness, unforgiveness, or low self-esteem define you. Instead, remind yourself that God created you to be a wise, determined, and beautiful woman—one who can diffuse tensions with grace, strength, and humility.

Prayer:

Abba Father, thank You for being merciful to me and being my help. Thank You for turning my fear into dancing and joy, allowing my heart to continue singing Your praises and not be silent (Psalms 30:10-12). I choose to trust You in everything I do, every decision I make because I know You are with me, holding me up with Your righteous right hand (Isaiah 41:10). You are my Shepherd, and I am the sheep of Your pastures, and I know You hold me close to Your heart and gently lead me through whatever situation or circumstances (Psalm 40:11) I am facing. Hold me tight Lord, and I will not be fearful even when bad decisions are made. Lord, I will praise You forever. In Jesus' Name, Amen.

ABOUT THE AUTHOR

Apostle Dr. Kimbrough, affectionately known as "Dr. K," has been married to Pastor Charles Kimbrough for 28 years in a blended family with four children. She accepted Christ at a young age in Tampa, Florida, and from her driveway, she began her feeding ministry, "House of Refuge Outreach Ministries," which started in Tampa, Florida, in 1978 and continues today in San Antonio, Texas.

Ordained as a Missionary at the age of 18 at Mount Olive Missionary Baptist Church, Dr. Kimbrough joined her mother in prison ministry, establishing her Prison Ministry. In 2012, she founded the Grace House of Refuge Community Development Corporation, a non-profit organization. Additionally, she founded Abba's Precious Jewels Ministry in 2005. Dr. K is renowned for her mentorship and serves as the Apostolic and Spiritual covering over various ministries in Tampa, FL, San Antonio, TX, and Africa.

She is a sought-after conference speaker and undertakes extensive international travel for foreign missions. Dr. Kimbrough serves on the National School Theology Alumni Association Board of Directors as Vice President and Regional Director. Her passion and mission are to create an atmosphere of inspiration, motivation, and innovation to facilitate personal and ministry growth for those called to spread the gospel of Jesus Christ across all nations. With the guidance of the Holy Spirit, she aims to bring total health and wholeness to all mankind.

- Awarded Honorary Doctorate for Community Leadership and Outreach 2012

- Earned Doctorate in Theology degree 2014,

- Chaplain Degree 2017

- Currently studying for her PhD in Mental Health Counseling

- VIP member of American Christian Counseling Association

- Ordained International Missionary 1978, Evangelist 1980, Ordained Pastor 2009, accepted my call & consecrated to the Apostolic 2015, Affirmation 2022.

- Professor with The National School of Theology, Dover, DE

CHAPTER 08

MASTERING THE MOMENT

Ebony A. Harris

66

"Now David was greatly distressed, for the people spoke of stoning him, because the soul of all the people was grieved, every man for his sons and his daughters. But David strengthened himself in the Lord his God."
-1 Samuel 30:6 (NKJV)

99

What do you do when your life crumbles before you despite your faithfulness to God?

In 1 Samuel 30, David faced a pivotal moment. His town, Ziklag, has been raided by the Amalekites, and his wives and children, along with the families of his men, have been taken captive. The men were so distraught that they spoke of stoning David, and even blamed him for their loss. David's response while in deep distress is instructive for us all. The scripture says, "David strengthened himself in the Lord his God" (1 Samuel 30:6). It's a heartbreaking scenario, and it's natural to feel overwhelmed, betrayed, and even question God's presence in your life. David's story doesn't end in despair and yours doesn't have to either. It's all about how you master the moment!

When everything seemed lost, David turned to God for strength. He didn't succumb to the despair or the blame of others. Instead, he sought God's guidance. David called for the ephod, a priestly garment used for seeking divine direction, and inquired of the Lord whether he should pursue the raiding party. God answered him, "Pursue, for you shall surely overtake them and without fail recover all" (1 Samuel 30:8).

In moments of utter despair, when life feels like it's falling apart despite our faithfulness, we can draw from David's example. Strengthen yourself in the Lord. This means pouring out your heart to Him, seeking His guidance, and holding onto His promises. It's about shifting your focus from the devastation to the One who has the power to restore.

David's story teaches us that God's faithfulness is not always about preventing hardships but about His presence and guidance through them. God didn't prevent the Amalekite raid, but He provided a path to recovery. David and his men pursued their enemies, and just as God promised, they recovered all that was taken. Not only did they retrieve their families and possessions, but they also gained additional spoils from the Amalekites (1 Samuel 30:18-20). God gave them greater!

The parallel here is profound. When you face your own Ziklag moments—when your life seems to be in ruins despite your faithfulness—remember that God is with you. Lean into Him. Seek His guidance with a heart ready to obey. Trust that His promises are true, and His plans are to give you a hope and a future (Jeremiah 29:11).

Mastering the most difficult moments in life involves a deep reliance on God. It means believing that, like David, you can recover all and more if you remain faithful and follow His lead.

It's not about avoiding challenges but about facing them with the assurance that God's power is made perfect in our weakness (2 Corinthians 12:9). When you strengthen yourself in the Lord and step forward in faith, you align yourself with His divine plan, and you, too, will experience restoration beyond your imagination.

So, take heart and master the moment. Your Ziklag is not the end; it's the place where God's promise of recovery and abundance begins.

Prayer:

Father, in the midst of my darkest moments, just as David turned to You in his time of distress, I ask that You help me to strengthen myself in You. Remind me of Your promises and help me to trust in Your unfailing love and faithfulness. Guide me on the path to recovery and restoration and give me the courage to face my challenges with confidence in Your power. May I lean on You, knowing that You are my refuge and strength, an ever-present help in trouble. Help me to master these difficult moments, trusting that Your plans for me are good and full of hope. In Jesus' name, I pray. Amen.

ABOUT THE AUTHOR

Ebony A. Harris is the founder of Empowering Lives Institute LLC, a transformative organization dedicated to helping women take control of their lives by fostering strength and confidence. Specializing in the mental, emotional, and spiritual development of women, Ebony utilizes techniques of inner healing and soul care to guide her clients toward profound personal growth.

As a Speaker, Author, Mental Health Strategist and Coach, Ebony brings a wealth of knowledge and experience to her engagements. Professionally, she is a Registered Nurse with over a decade and a half of experience in the mental health field. Her extensive career as a Mental Health Nurse, coupled with her rigorous training in Inner Healing, provides a solid foundation for her life's work.

Ebony's passionate speaking engagements carry a powerful message of healing and hope for those affected by mental illness and trauma. She draws on her professional expertise and personal journey of overcoming multiple traumas to connect deeply with her audience. Ebony believes her life's purpose is to heal and deliver a hurting generation, feeling called to her mission "for such a time as this."

Through Empowering Lives Institute LLC, Ebony continues to impact lives, empowering women to achieve mental and emotional well-being, reclaim their power and walk confidently in purpose.

CHAPTER 09

YOU CAN MAKE IT

Connie D. Rogers

> **"** *"For I know the thoughts that I think toward you, says the LORD, thoughts of peace and not of evil, to give you a future and a hope. Then you will call upon Me and go and pray to Me, and I will listen to you. And you will seek Me and find Me, and when you search for Me with all your heart. I will be found by you, says the LORD, and I will bring you back from your captivity; I will gather you from all the nations and from all the places where I have driven you, says the LORD, and I will bring you to the place from which I cause you to be carried away captive."*
> **-Jeremiah 29:11-14 (NKJV)**
> **"**

Have you ever felt like you couldn't make it? The truth is, we all experience these defeating thoughts at some point in our lives. But no matter what you've been through, are going through, or your current age, no one is exempt from life's challenges. Remember, defeat is not in you. Don't let life drag you down as if there is no hope. Instead, focus on God, keep your mind on positive things, and refresh yourself for new beginnings.

Each day and every moment offer a chance to start fresh with the grace, mercy, and peace of God.

Avoid dwelling on negative people, situations, and issues. Rise above them because you can make it. Don't let these matters keep you stuck in a rut of negativity and defeat. God has an abundance of promises and blessings ready to flow freely and bountifully into your life. Believe again by faith. Take a moment to reconsider your goals and aspirations because you are capable of achieving success in every area of your life. Rise up—you can make it.

Prayer:

Lord, I thank You for being an awesome God who reigns from heaven above with all wisdom, power, and love. I am grateful for the promise in Jeremiah 29:11-14, which assures me that You have a plan for my life and that I can make it. You are the King of Kings and the Lord of Lords. You are Almighty and wonderful. I can do all things through Christ Jesus, who gives me strength. I will not rely on my own understanding, but I will acknowledge our Lord and Savior, Jesus Christ. I believe there is a higher plan for my life, and I will pursue it, accomplish it, and reach it now. I call forth those things that are not yet as though they were, and I press towards the mark of the higher calling in Christ Jesus' name. I am determined to excel in every area of my life. Thank You, God, for being with me, never leaving me nor forsaking me. I can make it—whether it's being a caregiver, a great employee, a loving wife, a supportive mom, showing kindness, living a sanctified life, or overcoming depression. I claim what I say in Jesus' name, AMEN! Thank You, JESUS!

ABOUT THE AUTHOR

Connie D. Rogers, a dedicated Woman of God, has been a Senior Legal Administrative Assistant in the oil and gas industry within the Houston, Texas Metropolitan area since 2008. She holds a BS Degree in Business Integrated Supply Chain and Operations Management from the University of Phoenix and an AAS Paralegal Degree from the Center for Advanced Legal Studies. Originally from Bryan, Texas, Connie now resides in Missouri City, Texas with her mother and two children, Spencer (23) and A'Lyss (18), who regard her as a blessed figure in their lives.

Since 2022, Connie has been actively involved with Hope Renewed Global (HRG), participating in the Woman Arise Conferences in Austin, Texas in 2022 and 2023, and plans to attend the 2024 Woman Arise Conference in San Antonio, Texas. She also engages in the HRG Monthly 21-day Prayer Challenge, a Bible-based initiative that has significantly enhanced her sense of hope.

Connie's interests include spending time with God, family, and friends, as well as praying, mentoring, caring for her plants, exercising, and traveling.

CHAPTER 10

TAKE UP YOUR PROMISE

Apostle Latonia Moore

Have you ever experienced a portion of life when your needs were met in one area while simultaneously depleted in another quadrant of your life? Have you ever experienced a time when your resources, talents, and strategies worked well for others, yet did not resolve matters for you?

2 Kings 4:8-37 tells the account of a prominent and influential Shunamite woman who used her resources to construct an upper room for the prophet Elisha, providing him a place of refreshing when he passed through town. When Elisha asked what could be done on her behalf, the Shunamite woman informed him that she was among her people, in peace, and had no need for an advocate or favors. It was at that moment that Elisha's servant, Gehazi, reminded the prophet that she had no children. Elisha prophesied that she would embrace a son. According to the prophet's words, the Shunamite woman bore a son as promised. However, he later died.

Somewhere in life, we've all been like the Shunamite woman, when rejecting the promise(s) of God seems easier than receiving them. There has been a place in time when past efforts have served as legitimate reasons for not trusting an unknown probability.

It's then that we'd much rather decline the promise than be deceived into thinking that we can birth it, embrace it, or steward it.

What do you do when the thought of losing the promise is greater than the Word itself? How do you position yourself when the Word has been made flesh yet dies? What do you do when the business that you started isn't flourishing? What do you do when you're confident that God promised it, yet there's no sign of life?

Like the Shunamite, declare that "It is well." Run to the Giver of Life—God, your Father. Know that God cannot lie and put Him in remembrance of what He has spoken. Put Him in remembrance of His promises. Be reminded that you've built an altar—an upper room if you will. It is in this place of prayer that promises are not only reasoned but resurrected.

Recall to mind the various passages of scripture where lives were revived, restored, and resurrected. The God of yesterday is the God of today. He has not changed nor is there respect of persons with God (Romans 2:11). If He did it before, He can do it again!

As with the damsel spoken of in Matthew 9, your promise is not dead, but alive. Regardless of the report, how long it's been, or what the onlookers are saying—speak to it, prophesy over it, and most importantly, TAKE IT UP!

Prayer:

Heavenly Father, thank You for everything that You have predestined for me before the foundations of the world. Thank You for everything that is written in the books concerning me. I receive the truth that according to Ephesians 2:10, I am created unto good works in Christ Jesus and that I'm going to walk in what You have preordained. I repent for rejecting Your Word(s) concerning me, spoken directly to me or by way of Your servant(s). Forgive me for responding as if my circumstances superseded or eradicated Your will for my life. I stand in faith, declaring that Your promises concerning me are 'Yes'; therefore, I take them up and declare Your goodness. In Jesus' Mighty Name, Amen.

ABOUT THE AUTHOR

Apostle Latonia Moore accepted the call to preach as a teenager and was publicly affirmed as an apostle in 2009. She is often sought as a conference speaker, strategist, and [leadership] trainer. Apostle Moore enjoys community service and is on the Board of Directors for Resources for Women - a non-profit, Pro-Life agency. Professionally, Apostle Moore is a REALTOR®, and is a member of the San Antonio Board of REALTORS®.

Apostle Moore is the Senior Leader of Victorious Life Christian Center in San Antonio, Texas and is the founder of Kingdom Ambassadors Alliance, LLC - a ministerial alliance for churches, ministries, and marketplace leaders.

Apostle Moore has been married to her high school sweetheart since 1989. Four children, 1 grandchild and 3 GODchildren have blessed their union.

CHAPTER 11

MANIFESTED PROMISES

Mary J. Watkins

Did you know there are over 7,000 promises in the Bible? It's like having the answers to a test from the person who created the test. The real question is: Do you believe in the author of the book and the words on the pages? God once asked me, "Do you believe in Me as much as you believe in your mom?" My mom was never one to lie to me; even when it was difficult, her words were truthful. I believed my mom, and I believe in the author of the Bible and His promises!

God established a covenant with mankind through Abraham (Genesis 17), which was reaffirmed through the gospel of Christ. Covenants are the backbone of the Bible. I was taught that we are created in the likeness and image of God, and that the same Spirit who raised Christ Jesus from the dead lives in us (Romans 8:11). Paul emphasizes this in Ephesians 1:19-20, stating that the same power used by the Father to raise Jesus from the dead is at work within us. This power is not only energy but also the authority by which we accomplish great things. God created by speaking things into existence, and since we are created in His image, we have been given the authority to do even greater works than Jesus (John 14:12). As spirit beings, we are fully capable of operating with the same level of faith as God. Ephesians 5:1 tells us to be imitators of God, just as children imitate their parents. To imitate God, we must speak and act like Him.

God's Word is already established in the heavens, and He will keep His promises. So, what will you say about your situation? Words have the power to bring either victory or defeat. God is not creating anything new; it is up to us to speak His Word aloud, putting it into the atmosphere to renew our minds and reprogram our hearts.

Hebrews 11 (Amplified) reminds us: "Now faith is the assurance (title deed, confirmation) of things hoped for (divinely guaranteed), and the evidence of things not seen [the conviction of their reality—faith comprehends as fact what cannot be experienced by the physical senses]."

In conclusion, find scriptures related to your situation and release your faith through your words. Declare and decree what the Lord says, take action, and believe in God's Word, no matter what!

Prayer:

Father God, this is the day You have made, and I will rejoice in it. Your Word is a lamp unto my feet and a light unto my path; guide me in the right direction. Holy Spirit, You are the help I need to stay focused on Your promises. In Jesus's name, Amen.

ABOUT THE AUTHOR

Mary Joann Watkins is a devoted Christian, wife, mother, and grandmother with over 35 years of experience in healthcare, ministry, and community service. Her education from McNeese State University and Texas Southern University has provided a strong foundation for her professional and personal endeavors.

Throughout her nursing career, Mary has worked in diverse healthcare settings, including the Louisiana Department of Public Health, Houston Methodist Hospital, The Dow Chemical Company, and currently, the Houston Independent School District. Her role allows her to use her professional platform to share her faith and inspire others to dream big, making a significant impact on those around her. Additionally, she and her husband Ivory have successfully operated a catering business in Houston for over twelve years.

As a servant leader, Mary is actively involved in ministry, contributing to music, church leadership, and community projects. She is passionate about teaching future generations how to build a relationship with God, foster strong family units, and lead purpose-filled lives.

In her free time, Mary enjoys baking, reading, traveling, and spending quality time with family and friends. Her enthusiasm and joy are truly infectious, and she remains a dedicated evangelist, believing firmly in God's love for all mankind.

Contact Info: nuvisionconcepts@gmail.com

CHAPTER 12

HOPE AFTER THE TWELVE

Apostle Temico Myers

As we look at the life of the woman with the issue of blood, we can see ourselves through her experiences. We've all faced health issues, rejection, lost relationships, financial struggles, and feelings of unworthiness. Sometimes, we've isolated ourselves because of these challenges, many of which were beyond our control. But it is safe to include that each of us has endured some form of hardship.

God reaches us through the testimonies of others and various other sources, giving us glimpses of victory through our hearing. Whether we read the Word of God or hear a sermon at church, it is crucial to listen intently when God speaks.

The Word tells us that the woman with the issue of blood heard of Jesus. Here's a reminder that faith comes by hearing. I pose a question to you today: "Are you in a place where you can hear?" While we are going through trials, we need to hear what God is saying about our lives. If we never hear, will we ever move forward? Know that we will never be left alone or forsaken. Therefore, the answer lies in our hearing. Sometimes, God speaks in ways we may not expect, but will you listen?

Though the woman touched the hem of His garment, her healing didn't come from the touch itself but rather from her remarkable faith. We must place our faith in our Savior, Jesus Christ, and not in man, money, or any other god. When we act according to our own will, our resources may help, but they will never heal or deliver us. To be healed and made whole, we must go to Jesus because He is our only hope.

Her twelve-year issue brought hope to a man named Jairus, who needed healing for his daughter. Similarly, your issue may bring hope to another. Many may watch as you endure hardships, and not understand how or why. You can be sure that a heart turned toward God will bring you through any situation victoriously.

Our heart posture means everything, even in the toughest times. When your cry reaches God, He searches your heart. Responding the right way brings hope, peace, and freedom. As God gives you peace and freedom, others will receive the same through your testimony. Hearing allows them to have hope and by sharing this hope, others will know that the same strength that brought you through will bring them through as well.

Your issue is the very thing used to grow your faith and will be what turns the hearts of others toward God. God loves you and there is hope after her twelve years of suffering. Imagine how many will receive hope after your trials.

Prayer:

Lord, I thank You for reminding me that there is hope in You. I trust and believe Your Word. Thank You for Your grace and mercy. Allow my life to be an example to others and one that draws them closer to You. You, Lord, are my refuge; I trust You always. Amen.

ABOUT THE AUTHOR

Apostle Temico Myers began her walk with the Lord at Morning Star Missionary Baptist Church in Winnfield, LA. She later joined Interfaith Haven of Love Ministries under the leadership of the late Apostle Shelly Barnes, where she built a solid foundation as a prayer warrior and served tirelessly in many other capacities. Recognizing her faithfulness, God elevated her to serve as Praise and Worship Team Leader, Youth Director, Bible Study Teacher, President of the Pastor Aide Committee, Armor Bearer, and more.

Apostle Myers attended the School of the Prophets from 2011 to 2013. She was ordained as an Elder in 2015 and installed as Co-Pastor in 2022.

Apostle Myers is also the Executive Officer of the Annual Freedom Is Conference, teaching individuals to walk in the freedom of God, and a cohort of the Raw War Evangelistic Ministry.

Apostle Myers has a diverse career spanning several occupations. As a licensed cosmetologist, she became the owner and operator of Yunek Designs Salon. She has also received certification as a Yoni Steam Practitioner, adding another valuable service for her clientele. Additionally, she is a reputable Mary Kay Consultant. Apostle Myers desires to see people as God sees them and strives to strengthen and encourage the body of Christ through the preached Word of God. Given her leadership abilities, faithfulness, and the anointing on her life, she was installed as Senior Pastor on September 9, 2023.

CHAPTER 13

THE TEN-DAY TURNAROUND

Kimberly Clayton-Harris

> **"** *"About ten days later, the Lord struck Nabal and he died. When David heard that Nabal was dead, he said, "Praise be to the Lord, who has upheld my cause against Nabal for treating me with contempt. He has kept his servant from doing wrong and has brought Nabal's wrongdoing down on his own head." Then David sent word to Abigail, asking her to become his wife. Abigail quickly got on a donkey and, attended by her five female servants, went with David's messengers and became his wife."*
> **—1 Samuel 25:38-39, 42** **"**

The number ten holds great biblical significance. It symbolizes the perfect cycle of events, the number of perfection and harmony, and is also synonymous with redemption. Abigail, a beautiful and intelligent woman, bore the burden of being married to Nabal, a mean, surly, and wealthy businessman whose name meant "foolish." 1 Samuel Chapter 25 reveals how the actions and death of this foolish man became the gateway to the blessings of God for His servants David and Abigail.

David and his men watched over and protected Nabal's interests at no cost to him. David sent his men with a note to Nabal asking him to be favorable toward his men. Nabal rejected the request with insults and turned the men away.

When David heard of this, he set out to kill all the males on Nabal's land. Without informing her husband, Abigail quickly prepared a sacrifice to protect the inhabitants of her house from David's wrath. Abigail met David on the road, quickly bowed before him, and petitioned him to forgive the actions of her foolish husband. With wisdom, she reminded him that his actions could delay God's promise of him ruling Israel. David accepted the offering, heeded the voice of wisdom, and spoke blessings over Abigail for keeping him from avenging himself with his own hands.

When Abigail returned home, Nabal was drunk from feasting. When he sobered up, she told him what she had done, and his heart failed him. Verse 38 says: "About ten days later, the LORD struck Nabal, and he died." After ten days, God turned it around, avenged David, and removed the burden of a foolish man from Abigail. David sent word asking Abigail to be his wife. Abigail quickly got on a donkey with her servants and left with David's men. Abigail was ready and prepared. Her preparation not only blessed her life but also blessed the lives of her servants. There is nothing in the scripture that says Abigail procrastinated; it took ten days for Abigail to quickly walk into her turnaround.

Prayer:

Thank you, Father, that perfect harmony is my portion. I stand on Your word, knowing that things are about to turn in my favor. I lay aside the weights of rejection, distraction, and disappointment. Create in me a clean and contrite heart. I bow my face to You, Father, as I make ready for service. Make me a voice and a vessel of wisdom. I submit my will to Your will, and I commit to value what You value. Thank You for redemption and wholeness coming into my life. I will intently prepare and be ready to walk into my season of quick turnaround. Selah. Amen.

ABOUT THE AUTHOR

Kimberly Clayton-Harris is a Licensed Master Social Worker (LMSW) with a deep passion for helping others. Born as the second of four children in Louisiana, she grew up in a devout Christian household led by her parents, Pastor David and Laura Clayton Sr. She is an Elder and Worship Leader at New Birth Ministries. After graduating with an Associate Degree in Applied Science in Business Technology, Kimberly's pursuit of knowledge led her to earn a bachelor's in psychology and a master's in social work. Currently serving as a Supervisor at Odyssey House Louisiana, she dedicates her time to supporting individuals in recovery.

In 2022, tragedy struck with the unexpected loss of her beloved husband Mario Sr., leaving an immense void in her life. Yet, through adversity and the darkest season of her life, Kimberly found solace in her faith, declaring that God had transformed her sorrow into strength and resilience.

Today, she stands as a beacon of hope, using her experiences to uplift and empower others who have faced life's challenges. She is thankful for the gift of bonus children from her deceased husband: Brittany, Maya, Sabrina, and Mario Jr. Despite her loss, she declares that God has been faithful to her and has given her beauty for ashes. Kimberly's resilience and faith serve as an inspiration to others who are facing challenges in their own lives.

CHAPTER 14

READY, SET...WAIT!

Dr. Jessica Maxwell

> " *"They that wait upon the Lord shall renew their strength, they shall mount up with wings as eagles, they shall run and not be weary, they shall walk and not faint."*
> **-Isaiah 40:31** "

Choosing to live for Christ and be transformed with a new mindset and restored soul requires us to get ready, get set, and wait.

Getting Ready: This phase involves repentance, studying the Word, praying, fasting, and intentionally shifting your perspective while controlling your emotions. Worship should be our first response to afflictions. Collectively, these practices build our spiritual muscles, preparing us for battle and freeing our souls from bondage. The Lord is always ready to hear from us and respond as we make ourselves ready (Isaiah 65:1). Since Christ suffered physical pain, we must be ready to suffer as well (1 Peter 4:1). The magnificent thing about our faithful God, El Emunah, is that He awaits to hear us speak His Word so He can intercede on our behalf (Jeremiah 1:12).

Although the afflictions of those living for God are innumerable, we have peace knowing He will give us victory over pain, distress, grief, sickness, and problems (Psalm 34:19). We must be ready to use God's Word to command our mornings to align with His plans, will, and way. Always be ready, even when it's inconvenient (2 Timothy 4:2).

Getting Set: Once you're "ready," prepare to get "set" by staying in position and maintaining the posture of readiness. Repeat this daily to help maintain your "set" position. Remember, God is omniscient and omnipotent, seeing and knowing all that we can't see. Perseverance, faith, and trust in God are required to maintain this posture. When you're "set," you'll go through each trial with a sense of joy (James 1:2). As you remain "set," God is preparing, pruning, and maturing you, shifting you from strength to strength, glory to glory, and faith to faith (2 Timothy 2:1).

Waiting: Waiting may be the hardest part if we rush, rather than "wait" to see the process working for our good (Romans 8:28). Although it's human nature to proactively find solutions to problems, we must intentionally deny our will for the will and way of God. During the "wait," we must endure, eagerly look for God, and expect Him to move on our behalf. Moving prematurely could reset the entire process.

In the "wait," our faith and strength are renewed. He mounts us as eagles to excel, ascend, and spring into action as soon as He says go! The "wait" helps increase our endurance. The longer you "wait," the longer you'll be able to run, which is necessary for the next level. Skipping the "wait" will prevent perseverance from happening and cause you to faint as soon as you hit go. Study the Word, trust God, yield your will, and wait. Ready, set... wait!

Prayer:

Father God, transform us into new creatures as we choose to yield our will to You and submit to Your way. As we choose to trust You in the wait, we have an expectation that You will intervene on our behalf. In due season, we shall reap our harvest as we choose not to faint in the wait. May our youth be restored like eagles as we choose to worship You in spirit and in truth. In Jesus' Name, Amen.

ABOUT THE AUTHOR

Dr. Jessica Maxwell, PhD, OTD, OTR, CEAS, ACUE is the Program Director and Associate Professor for the UIW entry-level OTD program. Dr. Jess has her Ph.D. in Higher Education Administration: Educational Leadership and her post-professional Doctorate in Occupational Therapy. She has over 12 years of experience as an occupational therapist. She also has over six years of higher education administration with emphasis on teaching, book publications, grant writing, scholarship, and program and curriculum development. Dr. Jess is the proud owner of ErgoMax Solutions, PLLC offering ergonomics assessments and evaluations to computer workers. She is married to her loving husband and Airman, Major Joshua Maxwell of 12 years and they have three miracle boys, Joshua (8), Jeremiah (6), and Jenesis (4).

Whether teaching within the classroom, meeting with faculty or clients, volunteering within the community, speaking to strangers, or ministering as a praise and worship leader within the church, Dr. Jess has a passion for giving and loving on God's people. She has a servant's heart with the desire to see people healed, delivered, and grow deeper relationships with God.

CHAPTER 15

IT'S ME O' LORD

Apostle Tamara Walker

> " "I will lift up mine eyes unto the hills, from whence cometh my help. My help cometh from the LORD, which made heaven and earth."
> **--Psalm 121:1-2** "

Prayer: Father, before I read today's devotion, help me to see and hear what You are speaking to me. May this time of reading bring me into harmony with You and align me with what You are doing, can do, and are willing to do according to Your will and purpose for my life. In Jesus' Name, Amen.

Sometimes in life, "Woe is me" becomes our reality! The encounters, disappointments, discouragement, and unexpected life-changing situations can drain us to the point where we feel like we have nothing left to give, do, or say.

Although we may have faced such situations and experienced those "Woe is me" moments, there is hope for restoration and healing! Many have found it and received it, and I believe that after reading this today, you will too.

It's in GOD! Isn't it amazing that restoration comes from our Heavenly Father, who will not withhold any good thing from us?

As Psalm 84:11 (NLT) declares, "For the LORD God is our sun and our shield. He gives grace and glory. The LORD will withhold no good thing from those who do what is right." God can breathe His breath into dry bones and cause them to live again, as stated in Ezekiel 37:5 (KJV): "Thus saith the Lord GOD unto these bones; Behold, I will cause breath to enter into you, and ye shall live."

When God breathes back into us, it's a restoration moment! Life shifts from "Woe is me, empty" to "Yes, it's me, restored!" The reality may have been that all hope seemed lost, faith felt depleted—but today, you can rejoice and embrace the beauty for your ashes!

Get ready and take this journey of faith as you are restored, renewed, and revived. Take a deep breath in and breathe out...do it again...one more time. May each breath cause you to feel God breathing back into you, reviving, renewing, replenishing, refreshing, and restoring you back to life in Jesus' Name!

Come back and live again with the joy of the LORD, for His joy will be your strength! Come back to life and pray again. Come back to life and worship again! Come back to life and trust GOD again. Hold onto Him.

Come back, man, woman, boy, or girl—come back! Life is waiting to see you show up, blossom, and shine bright in the earth! You are the salt and the light in this world, according to Matthew 5:13-14. You are valuable and a great asset in Christ for the Kingdom of God!

Remember:

- You are fearfully and wonderfully made.
- You were created in His image.
- He is our Father.
- He has brought you back to life!

Thank You, Father! In Jesus' Name!

Prayer:

Father, as I have read and received what You have poured out today, may this process continue throughout my entire day—mentally, physically, and spiritually. Thank You for reviving, restoring, and causing my countenance to change. In JESUS' Name! Amen, Amen, and Amen! Selah.

ABOUT THE AUTHOR

Apostle Tamara Walker, affectionately known as "BIRD," was born on May 3, 1979. She spent her childhood in Weimar, Texas, with her loving mother, Theresa Burley, and her brother, Tyrell Glenn. Tamara's mother taught her how to be a lady, while her two aunts played vital roles in her upbringing. Betty Jean Flowers instilled in her the importance of prayer, and Joyce Faye McMillian taught her to be a strong young woman. With the guidance of these three influential women, there was no room for deviation from the values they imparted. Tamara adored her mother and aunts, who have since transitioned to be with the Lord, and she is confident their legacy will live on through future generations.

On October 22, 2006, Tamara married the love of her life, Mr. John Walker Jr. She delights in the fact that her husband of 11 years is loving and supportive.

John encourages her to follow God's will, and when challenges arise, his favorite words of encouragement to her are, "Baby, just go in the mountains." Tamara strives to continue being a virtuous wife to her husband.

In 2007, Tamara made the life-changing decision to accept and receive Jesus as her Lord and Savior. This decision led to her deliverance, setting her free from the chains of wickedness that once held her in a sinful lifestyle. She gives all glory to God for His love and freedom.

Tamara lives by Revelation 12:11: "And they overcame him by the blood of the Lamb and by the word of their testimony, and they did not love their lives to death." She uses her own testimony, aligned with the Word, to help others see that God shows no favoritism. What He has done for her, He will surely do for others.

In 2008, Tamara was led by the Holy Spirit to start her own women's ministry, "Women Winning Souls." This Holy Spirit-filled ministry, ordained by God, aims to teach, train, and guide people toward discovering their true purpose and worth in Jesus Christ. The ministry also seeks to reveal God's endless love, mercy, and grace in the lives of its members.

On May 22, 2011, Tamara earned her Certificate of Ordination and License at The Tabernacle of Light Worship Center, where she served under Bishop R.A. Campbell of Houston, TX. This milestone propelled her further into her God-ordained calling.

In 2013, Tamara experienced a devastating loss when her mother and Aunt Faye passed away. This brought immense pain, but with the support of her family and her loving brother, she was able to move forward with God's help.

Tamara, determined not to give up, has also studied Biblical Counseling at The College of Biblical Studies in Houston, TX, and understands firsthand that God is a miracle worker. She remains optimistic about her future.

On July 9, 2017, Tamara was appointed as Pastor of Ebenezer Baptist Church in La Grange, Texas. She continues to carry out God's mission for Ebenezer, leading the congregation in proclaiming Jesus Christ as Lord and Savior, the only way to God through faith, as affirmed in John 14:6: "Jesus said unto him, I am the way, the truth, and the life. No man cometh unto the Father, but by me."

Tamara is a free-spirited individual who glorifies God above all else. Her heart is focused on saving souls, and she is aware of the divine mandate upon the Body of Christ to reach those who are lost, broken, and counted out. With her selfless, non-judgmental spirit and anointing, Tamara continues to make a significant impact on the lives of others.

CHAPTER 16

REBOOT

Tony Johnson

> **"**
> *"Do not remember the former things, nor consider the things of old. Behold, I will do a new thing."*
> **--Isaiah 43:18-19**
> **"**

Have you ever wondered why you are the way you are? How your habits were established, why you're susceptible to certain things, or why you hold certain views? To whom or what do you ascribe praise or blame for who you've become—for the finished, "mature" you, for better or worse?

In the book of Genesis, 1:27, it states that "God created mankind." Genesis 2:5-8 continues that "no shrub had yet appeared, and no plant had yet sprung up," and God "planted a garden in the east, in Eden; and there he put the man." Jeremiah 1:5 provides insight from the Father Himself regarding our origin and purpose: "Before I formed you in the womb, I knew you. Before you were born, I set you apart." Jesus reinforces this in John 17:16, declaring, "They are not of the world, even as I am not of it."

Yet, an alternate view in the world seeks to bind us to the flesh, challenging our intelligence, distorting our recollection of God's word, and corrupting the original programming of our minds—the constructs designed by the Creator to ensure good health, prosperity (3 John 1:2), and dominion (Genesis 1:28) for all our days.

Science teaches that psychological development starts in the womb and that the initial programming of one's soul (mind, will, emotions, and intellect) begins after conception, before taking a breath and prior to any natural exposure to our environments. Without consulting the Father or considering spiritual aspects, identities and purposes are assigned, and destinies are framed. This leads to years spent growing into a foreign identity, embodying characteristics of a name with no credibility beyond the earthly realm.

This divergence from what is recorded in heaven creates vulnerability in the soul, distorting memory and causing reliance on untrusted or corrupted sources for direction. This is similar to technology. When a device's memory is corrupted or leaks, it behaves unpredictably, causing unresponsiveness, system lag, and frequent crashes. However, these issues can be mitigated with a system reboot, which clears the memory and resets the device to its original configuration. Similarly, we can reboot and be restored. Isaiah 43:18-19 instructs, "Do not remember the former things, nor consider the things of old. Behold, I will do a new thing; now it shall spring forth." Suddenly, the path we are to take and the standard by which we are to live become clear. The old is no longer relevant to who we are called to be; we can no longer measure life against memory. Everything we knew is moot because we are restored to our original programming. Behold, all is new.

Prayer:

Heavenly Father, we reboot. Every borrowed belief, every inherited value, every habit learned in Egypt—everything about us that did not originate with You—we shed and start afresh. May we now be free of every carnal bondage and become all that is written of us in heaven. Amen.

ABOUT THE AUTHOR

Tony worships under the Apostleship of Latonia Moore at Victorious Life Christian Center, San Antonio, Texas, where he has served as the sound technician since 2015. He is a husband, a father, a brother, and a son. As one who has dealt with and overcome rejection, condemnation, and guilt, among other things, Tony diligently seeks wisdom and audaciously applies kingdom revelation to the many facets of life as they are entered.

Professionally, Tony is a retired Air Force veteran and Senior Operational Technology Cybersecurity Specialist at one of the nation's more prominent architectural and engineering firms. He has a Master of Science in Cybersecurity and is credentialed through the International Information System Security Certification Consortium, holding the elusive Certified Information Systems Security Professional Certification.

CHAPTER 17

WHEN GOD MAKES YOU OVER

Dr. Morella Ivey

> 66
>
> *"Remember ye not the former things,*
> *neither consider the things of old..."*
> **--Isaiah 43:18**
>
> 99

God certainly has a funny way of doing things. It takes the foolish things to confound the wise (1 Corinthians 1:27), but sometimes it's as if God makes things look worse before He allows them to become better. No matter how much you try to avoid it, sometimes that walk through the valley of the shadow of death is inevitable. Let me encourage you today—beauty will emerge!

God wants to do a complete overhaul in your life, and if you let Him, when He's done, YOU won't even recognize YOU! True restoration requires the transformative power that only comes from God, and these renovations require patience and faith. It may look like the contractor doesn't know what He's doing, but lo and behold, beauty eventually begins to emerge from something you never imagined.

And by the way, in case you were wondering, God does have plans for your life, and newness is awaiting your arrival. I'm talking about a divine reset. An encounter with the Father—a Jacob moment—you won't ever be the same. God wants to return you to a state of optimal condition so that you can become the you He intended you to be. However, this transformation requires complete trust and total submission.

We must posture ourselves before God so that He can transform us. There's a reset button that only He has access to, and as you journey through and allow God to order your steps, each step will unlock hidden treasures you never knew existed. Don't be afraid of the newness; instead, embrace it. Yes, you're out of your comfort zone, but trust the process. God wants to reset you, renew you, and restore every part of you. When you let go and let God, not only will you begin to see yourself differently, but ultimately you will begin to see God differently. It's time to rediscover the YOU God intended. The you that was called and chosen from the womb. The renewed you, minus the trauma. The restored you.

Newness is on the horizon, so find joy in the journey and let God do what He does best...make you over.

Prayer:

Father, I confess that I'm struggling to see Your plans for my life. I need You to help me! Increase my faith and grant me the strength to trust You in all things. God, I surrender to Your will for my life. Make me over and restore unto me the joy of my salvation. In Jesus' name, Amen.

ABOUT THE AUTHOR

Dr. Morella Ivey is an inspirational educator who dedicates her days to using her superpowers in the classroom, teaching young children and shaping the next generation. With a passion for empowering others, she serves as a Bible College professor at Safe Haven Interdenominational Bible College, where she pours into her students, encouraging them to live out their God-given purpose and potential while sharing the message of God's love and grace.

Known for her dynamic teaching and ability to make the Word of God come alive, Dr. Ivey brings a wealth of life experiences and knowledge to her ministry. She has traveled extensively throughout the United States, spreading the gospel and proclaiming the redeeming power of Jesus Christ. Passionate about the things of God, she is dedicated to seeing lives transformed through the truth of His Word.

Dr. Ivey currently resides in the beautiful state of North Carolina with the love of her life, Apostle Dr. Joseph Ivey. Together, they are the proud parents of five amazing young men. Utilizing her talents and resources to build God's kingdom, she partners alongside her husband as they pastor Greater Full Assurance International Ministries. In addition, Dr. Ivey is the CEO of Ivey's Anointed Creations and Events By Ivey, through which she continues to expand her impact and influence.

Dr. Ivey holds a Master of Education in Early Childhood Administration and a Doctorate in Ministry with a concentration in Deliverance Ministry. Her hope is that her life will be a true reflection of Christ and that her ministry will always bring glory to God.

CHAPTER 18

RADICALLY RESTORED

Joshua Maxwell

> 66 "As he traveled he approached Damascus, and suddenly a light from heaven flashed around him [displaying the glory and majesty of Christ]; and he fell to the ground and heard a voice [from heaven] saying to him, "Saul, Saul, why are you persecuting and oppressing Me?"" 99
> —Acts 9:3-4

Saul's first encounter with Christ was radically different; it was new, fresh, and unique. This encounter also presented Saul with a challenging revelation, one that was instrumental in his soul being restored.

Early in his childhood, Saul learned about the strictness of Jewish laws from a Pharisee named Gamaliel, a famous and well-respected Jewish teacher of the law.

Although Gamaliel believed in the coming of the Messiah, he did not believe Jesus was the Messiah. Pharisees saw Jesus as a lawbreaker, and since Saul was inculcated with such thoughts as an adolescent, he carried these sentiments into adulthood.

As an adult, Saul further displayed his disdain for Christians who broke Jewish laws without remorse. Saul even admitted in Acts 26:9-10 that he once believed it was his duty to oppose Jesus with all of his might. With the authority entrusted to him by the chief priests, Saul wreaked havoc in Jerusalem, forcing many believers into prison and casting his vote for others to be put to death.

Saul had an obsessive hatred towards Christians, anyone who belonged to The Way (in John 14:6, Jesus proclaimed He "is The Way, and The Truth, and The Life"). Consequently, for every Christian Saul found, persecution was their reward. Although Saul was tenacious and unyielding in his pursuit to persecute Believers, a single encounter with God changed the trajectory of his life forever! Saul's name means "desired." God knew what He placed inside of Saul, and He waited for an opportune time to draw out what He desired; Saul's soul and his temperament! The initiation of this opportune time became the genesis of the transformative experience that restored Saul's soul.

As he journeyed to Damascus to broaden his territory for pursuing and persecuting Believers, he would submit to the One he'd actually been persecuting, Jesus. In an instant, Saul was humbled and came to the realization that God is much greater than anyone and anything, including himself. Instantaneously, the foundational principles Gamaliel taught Saul were challenged and overturned, because in that moment, Saul realized Jesus was actually the Messiah. Without a moment's notice, God began the process to restore Saul's soul. The word "soul" in the Hebrew language is *nephesh* (neh-fesh), and it refers to a person's mind, will, imagination, and emotions (BlueLetterBible.com).

Similarly, temperament is "the combination of mental, physical, and emotional traits" a person embodies (Dictionary.com).

Saul's soul being restored can be further explored and explained through Psalm 23:2-3. In these passages of scripture, David says "2 He makes me lie down... He leads me... 3 He restores my soul." To lie down is "to accept without protest or opposition" (Dictionary.com). Restore means "to bring back into existence, reestablish, to bring back to a former, original or normal condition, to bring back to a state of health, soundness, or vigor" (Dictionary.com).
Immediately following his Christ encounter, Saul obeyed Jesus' instructions without protest or opposition; Saul was made to lie down. The men Saul once led had to lead him to an appointed place, and after reaching that place, Saul's soul was restored. Once Saul's soul was restored, things were different; radically different. His name changed from Saul to Paul, his focus shifted to following The Way, and Paul was now a Believer who pursued and converted non-believers into Believers—same temperament, different goal.

Prayer:

"Lord, help me to abandon my will for Yours! Abba Father, I willingly submit my ways to You, and ask that You make me over again. Restore Your love in me, God; make me radically different as only You can! In Jesus' name, Amen."

ABOUT THE AUTHOR

Joshua Maxwell is a native of St. Marys, Georgia. He is happily married to his amazing wife, Jessica, and together they have three wonderful children: Joshua Jr., Jeremiah, and Jenesis. Joshua takes great pride in his roles as a husband and father, and his family inspires him to continuously strive to be the best version of himself.

He is currently an active-duty member of the United States Air Force, where he has served for over twelve years. Joshua joined the military in obedience to instructions he received from God, and he carries out every assignment with excellence for God's glory.

At heart, Joshua is a worshipper. Leading others into God's presence through worship is one of his greatest passions. Ultimately, Joshua strives daily to walk in God's will for his life, to see the world through God's perspective, and to represent both God and his family well in everything he does.

CHAPTER 19

THE GOD OF RESTORATION

Lorine Jefferson

> 66 *"I will repay you for the years the locusts have eaten—the great locust and the young locust, the other locusts and the locust swarm—my great army that I sent among you. You will have plenty to eat, until you are full, and you will praise the name of the Lord your God, who has worked wonders for you; never again will my people be shamed."*
> **-Joel 2:25-26 (NIV)** 99

Restoration means bringing something back to its original state, and whatever we need restored can be found in the Word of God. When we stray from the path of righteousness and lean on our own understanding, we become disobedient. Losing our joy leads to losing our strength, for "the joy of the Lord is my strength." When we face disobedience, the things we hope for—jobs, dreams—seem to disappear. For God to restore what has been lost, we must repent of our wrongdoing and earnestly cry out to Him.

God's love is unconditional, and He is the ultimate Restorer. He will move us from a place of scarcity to abundance, from hunger to satisfaction.

He will restore our praise, bringing gladness and rejoicing to our hearts, music to our soul, and expressions beyond language. We should rejoice, pray, and thank God for what He is doing, has done, and will do. Praise shifts our focus to God. As we praise Him amid our problems, our troubles will diminish, for God can turn any bad situation into good.

We should praise God like never before for His restoration. As Psalm 150:1-6 (NIV) proclaims: "Praise the Lord! Praise God in his sanctuary; praise him in his mighty heavens. Praise him for his acts of power; praise him for his surpassing greatness! Praise him with the sounding of the trumpet, praise him with the harp and lyre, praise him with timbrel and dancing, praise him with the strings and pipe, praise him with the clash of cymbals, praise him with resounding cymbals. Let everything that has breath praise the Lord. Praise the Lord."

God is not only a Restorer of plenty, praise, and purpose but also a Restorer of protection. He will always protect us and be there for us. As Psalm 46:1 (NIV) states: "God is our refuge and strength, an ever-present help in trouble." He will uphold us and protect us with His righteous right hand. No matter what we are going through, we must hold on until our change comes. The Lord may not come when we want Him to, but He is always on time.

Prayer:

Father God, please restore my life—my health, joy, material blessings, soul, relationships, peace, faith, prayer life, and family. Thank You for being a God of restoration. Lord, bless me indeed, enlarge my territory, keep me from evil, and keep Your hand upon me. Restore everything I have lost. Amen! Amen! Amen!

ABOUT THE AUTHOR

Lorine Jefferson is a Licensed Nursing Home Administrator with over 20 years of experience in elderly care. Her professional responsibilities include managing the daily operations of her facility and ensuring that the organization remains aligned with its long-term goals and mission.

With a deep passion for caring for the aged and disabled, Lorine began her journey in caregiving by assisting her mother in caring for her grandmother at a young age. This early experience sparked a lifelong commitment to helping those who cannot help themselves, ensuring that they are treated with dignity and respect.

A dedicated member of Macedonia Missionary Baptist Church in Livingston, Texas, Lorine serves as the church clerk and is actively involved in various capacities.

She provides encouragement to families by reading resolutions during times of loss and assists with the church's financial aspects as a member of the administrative staff.

Lorine resides in Livingston, Texas, where she graduated from Livingston High School. She later earned a Bachelor's Degree in Business Management from the University of Phoenix. She has a daughter, a granddaughter, and a great-grandson.

In her personal time, Lorine enjoys reading her Bible, spending time with family, walking, traveling, and dining out. She is also looking forward to taking a cruise in the near future.

Lorine's passion remains in providing care for the aged and disabled, ensuring they are safeguarded from harm and treated with the utmost dignity and respect.

Her contact information is
lorinejeffersonn@gmail.com.

CHAPTER 20

BASIC RESTORATION

Kinshanna Fontenot

> 66
> *And be not conformed to this world: but be ye transformed by the renewing of your mind, that ye may prove what is that good, and acceptable, and perfect, will of God.*
> **-Romans 12:1-2**
> 99

The enemy attacks us emotionally, mentally, and spiritually because he knows that if he can control our thoughts and actions, he has control over us. We cannot act on anything until it first enters our minds.

I remember a time when I was in a spiritually dry place. Much had happened in the lives of those around me, which led me to question what God was doing. This uncertainty marked my dry season. The mental attacks from the enemy were overwhelming; I knew God, but I struggled to connect with His presence.

I found myself in a state where I couldn't feel God's presence. I was numb to His movement, unable to hear or receive His voice. All I knew was that I needed God's help to escape this stagnant place.

Eventually, I attended a conference with a group of women who loved God. During the event, a prayer line was called, and I went forward asking for prayer. I explained that while I could forgive others, I struggled to engage with them after the attack. That day, God used a woman of faith to speak truth into my life: I had not truly forgiven them. She provided me with instructions and a prayer to help heal my heart and love others as Christ loves them.

I can honestly say that God has restored my love for people, and I now see them through His lens. If you find yourself in a similar situation, ask God for forgiveness, request a renewal of your mind, and trust that He can restore you and help you love again. With a clean heart, right spirit, and sound mind, God will hear your prayers and withhold no good thing from you.

Prayer:

Father God, thank You for this opportunity to come before You. I ask that You cleanse my heart and renew my mind. Purify my thoughts and saturate my mind with Your thoughts so that I may think as You think. Help me to see things as You see them and to hear things as You hear them. Guide me to speak as You would have me speak. In Jesus' name, amen!

ABOUT THE AUTHOR

Kinshanna Fontenot was raised in the church, where she developed a deep connection with her faith and discovered her gift for singing. Known for her special selections as a soloist, Kinshanna's musical talents were recognized early on during her time at a local ministry in her hometown. Singing has been a passion of hers since childhood, and she continues to share her gift with others.

Kinshanna later married her church sweetheart, and together they have a beloved son who brings them immense joy. Her mission is to do God's will, remain steadfast in her faith, and touch people's lives through her music.

In addition to her musical endeavors, Kinshanna is a Master Social Worker who serves her community in various capacities. Her dedication to her profession and her passion for fulfilling her divine calling reflect her deep love for God and commitment to making a positive impact.

CHAPTER 21

A NEW LIFE

Pastor Cynthia Stallings

> 66
>
> *"He asked me, 'Son of man, can these bones*
> *live?' I said, 'Sovereign Lord, you alone know.'*
> *Then he said to me, 'Prophesy to these bones*
> *and say to them, "Dry bones, hear the word of*
> *the Lord! This is what the Sovereign Lord says*
> *to these bones: I will make breath enter you,*
> *and you will come to life."'*
> **—Ezekiel 37:3-5 (NIV)**
>
> 99

Have you ever felt as though you were in a dry place or a hopeless situation? Perhaps the challenges you face have interrupted your walk with the Lord, leaving you feeling spiritually barren. Proverbs 17:22 (NIV) says, "A cheerful heart is good medicine, but a crushed spirit dries up the bones." Where do you turn for help, hope, and healing? Can you truly be restored to a new life?

Paul writes, "If anyone is in Christ, he is a new creation. The old has passed away; behold, the new has come." This is not just renovation but a complete restoration.

Ezekiel spoke to the dry bones, commanding them to listen to the Word of the Lord. We must also listen and hear the Word of the Lord. The Spirit of God desires to breathe new life into our lifeless situations. We are called to put off our old selves, corrupted by deceitful desires, and to be made new in the attitude of our minds. We are to put on the new self, created to be like God in true righteousness and holiness.

First, we need to desire to rid ourselves of our sinful nature and former ways, forgetting what is behind us and pressing toward the mark of the high calling in Christ Jesus. By keeping our eyes on the Lord and not wavering in our faith, God will hear and answer our prayers. God's Word assures us that He will forget the past. Isaiah 43:18-19 says, "Forget the former things; do not dwell on the past."

When God restores our soul, there is a profound sense of peace and comfort. The Lord provides the restoration we need, and only He can do so. If you're experiencing disappointment or uncertainty, remember that Jesus came to give life abundantly.

God's Word is our source of renewal. John 1:4 states, "In Him was life, and that life was the light of men." Jesus refreshes and restores our hope. Psalm 23:3-4 says, "He refreshes and restores my soul." Isaiah 38:16 declares, "O Lord, by such things men live, and in all of them my spirit finds life. You restored me to health and let me live." The Lord is the stronghold of our lives; whom shall we fear?

Let the mind of Christ be in you. He can restore our mind, emotions, and spirit when we sing of the Lord's lovingkindness and declare His faithfulness. God is a restorer of life. Though we may feel dead, we shall live again.

Reflecting on transformation, I recall my grandmother offering me an old, dilapidated chair. Initially, I saw no worth or potential in it. However, with encouragement, I began to see beyond its flaws. After applying cleaner, polish, and paint, the chair was restored to beauty and comfort. Similarly, God's restoration reveals a beauty in us beyond what the eyes can see.

His presence assures us that He will never leave nor forsake us. Jesus Christ is the same yesterday, today, and forever. He never changes. Life and death are in the power of the tongue. We must speak life. The Bible teaches that we can have what we say. Therefore, we speak health, healing, happiness, and wholeness. We speak life into every dead situation. New life is found in being "in Christ" — united with Him through His death, burial, resurrection, and exaltation at the Father's right hand.

Prayer:

Dear Heavenly Father, we praise You for You alone are worthy of praise. Sovereign Lord, You restore my soul. My soul magnifies You, Lord. No situation is hopeless for You. Grant us a clean heart and mind, steadfastly focused on You. Thank You for the abundance of life and for renewing our hearts, spirits, and lives. Thank You for restoring new life within us, enabling us to serve others as You have served us. In Jesus' Name. Amen.

ABOUT THE AUTHOR

Pastor Cynthia Stallings, a resident of North Carolina, embraced the Lord at a tender age, becoming a devoted and gifted servant of God with an unwavering commitment to fulfilling His will. For 44 years, she has been the cherished wife of Pastor Curtis Stallings. A retired educator, she dedicated 33 years to the Perquimans County School System.

Educated with a Bachelor of Science in Education from Elizabeth City State University and a Master of Arts from East Carolina University. Pastor Cynthia was licensed and ordained as a pastor in 2002. Her service extends across various roles, including congregational care pastor and mentor to disciples.

Recipient of North Carolina's esteemed Order of the Long Leaf Pine Award, Pastor Cynthia has left an indelible mark through her exceptional service and outstanding contributions to both the state and her communities.

An ardent lover of music and worship, she finds solace in her quiet moments with the Lord, often sharing her talents as a psalmist and motivational speaker. Her radio segment, "On a Personal Note," has inspired many.

Beyond her Christian duties, Pastor Cynthia has actively participated in community affairs, serving on multiple boards, including the Perquimans County Library Board and Winfall Town Council.

Currently serving as an intercessor at New Life Covenant Southeast Church in Chicago, Illinois, under Pastor John Hannah's leadership.

Throughout her journey, Pastor Cynthia remains steadfast in giving glory and offering the highest praise to God.

CHAPTER 22

RESTORATION THROUGH FAITH

Kimberly Davis-Smith

> **66** [43] *And a woman having an issue of blood twelve years, which had spent all her living upon physicians, neither could be healed of any,* [44] *Came behind him and touched the border of his garment: and immediately her issue of blood stanched.* [48] *And he said unto her, Daughter, be of good comfort: thy faith hath made thee whole; go in peace.*
> **-Luke 8:43-44, 48** **99**

We all know the story of the woman with the issue of blood. She suffered with her ailment for twelve long years and had spent all her resources going to physician after physician, seeking a solution to her problem. She put all her faith into multiple doctors only to remain dissatisfied, not cured, and still broken. This story reminds me of when I struggled with my own health scare. I saw doctor after doctor seeking a solution only to remain disheartened and broken time and time again. I was told that the tumor in my abdomen was cancerous and that I should leave the teaching profession and expect radiation.

I exited his office keeping his diagnosis to myself and began to declare and decree that cancer was not my portion. I decided, just as the woman with the issue did, to give Jesus a try and put my faith in him instead. She knew that if she could just get through the crowd, if she could just touch the hem of his garment, she would be healed. I knew that if I gave my situation over to God, fully trusted him, and applied my faith, I would be made whole as well.

Weeks later, after the surgery, I was informed that the tumor was indeed noncancerous and that I would not need radiation. By having faith, I was able to be healed, just as the woman in the story. God can turn any situation around and not only restore you physically, but also mentally, emotionally, and spiritually.

In Luke 8:48, Jesus tells the woman to go in peace. According to Collins Dictionary, doing something in peace means to be physically relaxed and contented, not feeling any pain or unpleasant sensations. When we truly give everything over to God in faith, He will exhibit compassion, providing comfort and a peace like no other.

The story of the woman with the issue of blood is mentioned in Matthew 9:20-22, Mark 5:25-29, and Luke 8:40-48. The repetition of its mentioning lets us know the importance of the story and the role faith plays in receiving your breakthrough and healing. She ran out of money, she ran out of resources, but she didn't run out of faith, and because of this her faith made her whole!

Prayer:

Father God, I come before you now giving you all the honor and praise for who you are. Forgive me for not trusting you in every area of my life and for not exhibiting faith when I should have. I thank you for what you have already done in my life, and I thank you in advance for your healing from the top of my head to the soles of my feet. Healing is my portion, and I shall be made whole physically, mentally, emotionally, and spiritually. In Jesus' name, amen."

ABOUT THE AUTHOR

Kimberly Davis Smith is a native of Natchitoches, Louisiana, who has been happily married for over 23 years. Together with her spouse, she has six children ranging in age from 27 to 19 and six grandchildren. With over 16 years of experience as an educator and more than 10 years as a well-known fitness instructor in her community, Kimberly has made significant contributions both professionally and personally.

She is an active member of New Light Baptist Church in Natchitoches, where she serves as the Youth Director and Sunday School teacher under the leadership of Pastor Cynthia Lee Cole. Kimberly enjoys decorating, traveling, praise dancing, and spending quality time with friends and family. She is passionate about sharing her testimony of God's love, healing, and restoration with others.

One of Kimberly's favorite quotes is, "Be the change you want to see," and her go-to scripture is Isaiah 41:10 KJV: "Fear thou not; for I am with thee: be not dismayed, for I am thy God: I will strengthen thee; yea, I will help thee; yea, I will uphold thee with the right hand of righteousness."

CHAPTER 23

YOUR FAITH MADE YOU WHOLE

Christina Jackson

> **❝**
>
> *"And He said to her, 'Daughter, your faith has made you well. Go in peace.'"*
> **--Luke 8:48 NKJV**
>
> **❞**

The woman with the issue of blood exemplifies unwavering faith. Despite her suffering and the obstacles she faced, she persevered and pressed through the crowd. Her story teaches us the importance of maintaining faith, regardless of our circumstances. We, too, must keep pressing, pushing, and praying, while holding onto our faith. Storms may come, but they are temporary. They are here to teach us, mold us, and refine our character and integrity.

Had the woman not gone through her trial, she might not have discovered her inner strength or learned to depend on God. We cannot rely solely on our own strength, but through Christ, we can do all things (Phil. 4:13). God desires to restore us, make us whole, and renew our minds, bodies, and souls.

Allow Him to cleanse you from all that is unclean (2 Corinthians 5:17). Approach God with confidence, knowing that He already knows everything about you. Let Him make you new; your past is gone, and you can start anew in Him.

We may not know exactly when or how our breakthrough will come, but we must believe that it will happen. Even when situations seem bleak, remain steadfast in your faith, trusting that God will bring about resolution. Faith moves God, so we must move in faith. Even a faith as small as a mustard seed can lead to miracles with God's power. Whatever your issue may be today, surrender it to Jesus and let your faith bring healing. God wants to heal your soul.

Prayer:

Father, in the name of Jesus, I ask You to touch everyone dealing with issues in their lives. Your Word tells us in 1 Peter 5:7 to cast all our cares on You because You care for us. Right now, we give You all that concerns us: our families, finances, health, minds, homes, and hearts. We thank You for our faith in You, knowing that faith without works is dead (James 2:14). We look to the hills, knowing our help comes from the Lord. Even through pain and disappointment, let us keep our eyes on You and our trust in Your hands. Grant us the endurance to run this race with perseverance. We give You all honor and glory for what You have done, what You are doing, and what You will do in our lives. Thank You for our healing and deliverance. As the Lord is our Shepherd, we shall not want, and He restores our souls for His name's sake. In Jesus' Name, Amen.

ABOUT THE AUTHOR

Christina Jackson-Wright's journey has been marked by resilience, compassion, and unwavering faith. After graduating from high school, she began her professional path by attending Job Corp in San Marcos, TX, where she obtained her CNA license. She later relocated to Houston, TX, for a time.

In 2000, Christina's life took a significant turn when she became pregnant by her late husband, Donald Jackson Jr. Together, they welcomed one son and two daughters—Dalen, Deseray, and Desire Jackson—who brought immense joy and inspiration to Christina's life.

Despite the joys of motherhood, Christina faced profound losses that tested her strength and faith. In 2010, her beloved mother passed away after a battle with cancer.

Christina, along with her family, provided comfort and support to her mother's devoted caregivers until her passing on March 26, 2010.

Further heartache came in 2019 when her brother, Bradley, succumbed to cancer and other illnesses. Through these trials, Christina remained steadfast in her faith, finding solace in God's presence and drawing strength from her loved ones.

Now residing in Schulenburg, TX, Christina is a faithful member of Greater Macedonia Church in Weimar, TX. She serves as a beacon of hope and compassion in her community. Employed at Park View Nursing Home, she continues to extend her nurturing spirit to those in need, embodying the values of love, resilience, and faith that define her remarkable life.

CHAPTER 24

FROM BENT OVER TO STANDING TALL

A JOURNEY OF TRIUMPH AND TRANSFORMATION

Montrell A. Hawkins, MSL

> **"**
>
> *Now He was teaching in one of the synagogues on the Sabbath. And behold, there was a woman who had a spirit of infirmity eighteen years, an was bent over and could in now way raise herself up. But when Jesus saw her, He called her to Him and said to her, "Woman, you are loosed from your infirmity." And He laid His hands on her, and immediately she was made straight, and glorified God.*
> *–Luke 13:10-13 NKJV*
>
> **"**

During the Sabbath, while Jesus was teaching in a synagogue, He encountered a woman who had been afflicted by a spirit for eighteen years. This condition left her bent over, restricting her ability to stand upright and see clearly.

Her physical ailment profoundly affected her sense of self, reducing her to an unidentified figure—was she known as Lisa, Tonya, Mia, or simply as the woman who was always bent over?

In society, we often label individuals with titles such as "teenage mothers," "divorcees," "drug addicts," or "alcoholics." Similarly, questions may arise about the cause of her spinal deformity, speculating on the life experiences that led to her state. For eighteen years, she endured the pain and struggles of her condition, finding no relief despite her unwavering faith.

What did Jesus do? He offered hope amid her circumstances, reaching beyond her name, identity, and physical condition. The remarkable part is that despite not being able to see Jesus, she somehow knew He was calling her. With humility and courage, she approached Him, knowing that all eyes were on her. Despite being self-conscious, she answered the call.

Jesus' compassion was evident as He laid His hands on her and declared, "Woman, you are set free of your infirmity." His words and touch defied cultural norms, granting her both freedom and dignity. She stood up straight, looked at Jesus, and glorified God, her years of suffering transformed into joy and triumph. Her spiritual wounds were healed as she embraced her new identity as a daughter of the King, giving thanks for her journey of transformation by standing tall with her hands raised toward heaven.

Prayer:

Our Father, in challenging times, when we face discouragement and battles, both internal and external, we find solace in You, the "Author and Finisher of our Faith." Jesus, our protector, is always by our side. We are grateful for Your power to transform our perspectives and strengthen our inner resolve.

Your acknowledgment of our vulnerabilities and the restoration of our resilience fills us with gratitude. We lift our voices in praise and glorify Your name, seeking strength through our Lord and Savior, Jesus Christ. In Jesus' name, Amen.

ABOUT THE AUTHOR

Montrell Hawkins is a proud native of Madison, Florida, and a devoted mother of four children: Makeela, Mahogani, Marcus Jr., and Maliyah. A lifelong follower of Christ, Montrell is an active member of Shiloh Missionary Baptist Church in Madison, FL, where the community embraces the motto, "We walk by faith and not by sight."

Montrell's educational journey began with a strong foundation from Madison County Public Schools, leading to her achievements at Grand Canyon University, where she earned a Master of Science in Leadership and a Bachelor of Science in Applied Management. She is currently pursuing a Doctor of Business Administration in Management from St. Thomas University, reflecting her dedication to continuous personal and professional growth.

In her role as a Finance Assistant for Payroll and Employee Benefits at Madison County District Schools, Montrell is valued for her meticulous attention to detail, leadership skills, and financial expertise. Her colleagues appreciate her commitment to excellence and her willingness to go above and beyond.

In her leisure time, Montrell enjoys spending quality moments with her children, friends, and family, attending basketball games, cruising, savoring delicious cuisine, and shopping. Above all, she finds profound joy and comfort in reading her Bible, listening to praise and worship music, attending fellowship, and reflecting on its teachings. Her favorite scripture, Jeremiah 29:11, reassures her of God's love and His plans for a hopeful future.

CHAPTER 25

GOD CAN UNBEND YOU

Evangelist Cheryl Bridgewater

> **"**
>
> *"And there was a woman who had a spirit of infirmity eighteen years, and was bent over, and could in no way lift herself up. When Jesus saw her, He called her to Him and said, 'Woman, you are loosed from your infirmity.' And He laid His hands on her, and immediately she was made straight and glorified God."*
> **--Luke 13:11-13**
>
> **"**

In this passage, we encounter a woman who suffered not merely from physical illness, but from a spirit of infirmity—meaning a demonic presence was behind her suffering. Bent over and unable to straighten herself, she had endured this condition for eighteen long years. This physical state symbolizes deeper struggles; perhaps you, too, have faced a period where you felt spiritually, mentally, or emotionally unable to stand upright, feeling trapped in a cycle with no visible solution or breakthrough.

This woman's condition was more than a physical ailment; it represented years of unresolved issues, setbacks, and emotional scars. You might have endured verbal, physical, or emotional abuse, or faced dysfunctional family dynamics that left deep imprints on your soul. Yet, today, you are declared free. Just as Jesus saw the woman and called her to Him, He sees you and calls you to receive His touch. Hear His voice and be set free. Allow God's hand to touch you, bringing immediate transformation and lifting you from the burdens that have kept you bowed down.

As John 8:36 states, "If the Son therefore shall make you free, you shall be free indeed." Through the divine and unlimited power of the Holy Spirit, I declare that you are no longer bound but set free!

I encourage you today to embrace your freedom from diminished capacity, weaknesses, and emotional frailties. Whatever devastation you have experienced, be assured that help is coming through the power of God Almighty. Ignore the judgments and questions of others about your situation. Instead, focus on the truth that God is removing you from past demons, negative influences, and obstacles to prosperity and peace. Now, glorify God for your deliverance and celebrate your newfound freedom!

ABOUT THE AUTHOR

Evangelist Cheryl Brownfield Bridgewater is a native of Baton Rouge, Louisiana, and a former resident of Winnfield, Louisiana. She currently resides in Natchitoches, Louisiana. As a devoted mother, she has three sons: two biological, Gerry and Jeremy, and a godson, Mike, whom she has lovingly nurtured and cared for.

Ms. Bridgewater is a cherished member of Mt. Pilgrim Baptist Church in Clarence, Louisiana, where she serves under the spiritually profound and anointed leadership of Pastor James B. King, Jr. At her church, she holds multiple roles, including Women's Ministry Director, Director of the Pastor's Aide Committee, and Minister of Music.

Professionally, Ms. Bridgewater is an educator in the Natchitoches Parish School System. She is dedicated to instilling a positive mindset in her students, helping them achieve their highest academic and social potential.

Her passions include public speaking, music, reading, and writing.

Evangelist Cheryl Brownfield Bridgewater has navigated and overcome numerous spiritual and physical adversities. Her unwavering trust in God and her commitment to transparency have been cornerstones of her life. She embraces accountability and responsibility, remaining steadfast and unmovable in her faith. Her dedication to spiritual growth and integrity is evident in her life's work. With God as her foundation, she is destined for great accomplishments.

CHAPTER 26

GOD GRANTS RESTORATION FOR LOSSES AND BESTOWS PROTECTION AND FORTITUDE

Denetrica Green-Hatten

> **"** *"The Lord himself goes before you and will be with you; he will never leave you nor forsake you. Do not be afraid; do not be discouraged."*
> **–Deuteronomy 31:8** **"**

There are times when I sit back and speak to God with the utmost respect. "God, I have lost an enormous amount of material things. I have lost several loved ones who played vital roles in my life. As a young teenage girl, I lost my mother at the age of 14. I was raised by my father and older siblings. There was a deep hurt and anger I couldn't explain. I had one pressing question for God: why did You take my mother away from me? This was such a crucial time in a teenage girl's life—I needed her. I longed for my mother to teach me how to become a woman she would be proud of.

Through God's grace, mercy, and guidance, my father and older siblings stepped in to raise me. My sisters became like mothers to me, taking on that role. I must also mention my one and only brother-in-law, a great man who supported me both in my successes and in my struggles. He would always tell me that if I put my mind to something, I could do it. He was my personal cheerleader. When I needed to talk, he would just sit and listen, offering only constructive criticism, which I appreciated because it helped build my confidence.

After graduating from high school, I moved to Houston, TX, where my sisters lived. I decided to attend vocational school and study Medical Assisting. I completed the nine-month course and was employed at a doctor's office. Later that year, I met a young man, and we fell in love and had two children. However, we were not equally yoked, and I faced many challenges, especially in raising my oldest child. I endured things I never imagined a person could go through. I had to step back and ask God, "What am I doing? This isn't anything I was raised around, and it all feels so foreign to me." It was a total disappointment—a lost relationship.

I remember one day when I was running errands with my sisters and returned to my apartment to find an astonishing sight—my living room was completely empty. All my furniture was gone. This was the furniture I had worked extra hours to buy, and now it was gone. It was another loss, and an eye-opener. I prayed, asking for God's help to guide me in making the best decisions for myself and my children.

Around this time, my oldest brother, who had just remarried, asked me to come to Dallas to stay with his teenage daughters while he and his wife went on their honeymoon. I wasn't too excited about going because I had so much on my mind. But after talking with my oldest sister, I realized it might be a good opportunity for a change of scenery and time to reflect on my life.

After some contemplation, I decided to take my brother's offer and went to Dallas. While there, I spent time with my nieces and enjoyed the change of atmosphere. A week later, my brother and his wife returned.

I continued to seek God's guidance through prayer, and eventually, I felt He gave me the answer. I decided to stay in Dallas instead of returning to Houston. I must admit, there were ups and downs, but God never left me or my children. In time, I met my husband, and we have been married for 32 years. Of course, we all face life's unexpected valleys and occasional hills.

In June 2016, we experienced a traumatic event—a home fire. We lost everything. I thought I was having a nightmare and kept asking God to wake me up. But God brought us through, showing that there is nothing He cannot do. He is so generous in granting restoration for all losses and providing His arms of protection.

Prayer:

In the name of Jesus, I humbly come before You, Heavenly Father, seeking Your guidance and grace. I ask that anyone who comes across this message gains the insight and comfort that, despite any losses they may face, You, our merciful God, are always there to restore, protect, and provide for us. Amen.

ABOUT THE AUTHOR

Denetrica Green-Hatten resides in the Dallas-Fort Worth area. She has been married for 30 years and has 3 children and 5 grandchildren. Originally from Southwest Louisiana, Denetrica has been living in Texas for over 30 years. She has a deep love for people and enjoys interacting within a diverse community. One of her favorite hobbies is cooking, and she is the owner of E'llee's Cajun Dishes. Following in her mother's footsteps, Denetrica specializes in preparing delicious Cajun dishes. She finds great satisfaction in seeing the expressions on people's faces when they take their first bite of her food.

Later in life, Denetrica decided to further her education. She attended Ashford University online, where she earned a Bachelor of Science degree in Business Administration in May 2016. Shortly after, in June 2016, she began working for a local municipality, where she is still employed.

However, just after receiving her degree, Denetrica faced a devastating experience. Her family's home was destroyed by a fire, and they lost nearly everything, leaving them homeless. It was a very dark time for Denetrica and her family. During this difficult period, they received assistance from the Red Cross, friends, and family.

Despite these challenges, Denetrica sought God's guidance and prayed about whether to continue her education. She decided to pursue a Master's in Public Administration, though there were times when the stress made her doubt whether it would work out. Yet, with God's help, she persevered and graduated in 2018 with her master's degree. Denetrica has been employed with the local municipality since June 2016 and continues to serve in that role today.

CHAPTER 27

HE RESTORES ALL

Suelynn Grace Holloway

> " *"If your heart is broken, you'll find God right there; if you're kicked in the gut, He'll help you catch your breath."*
> **-Psalm 34:18** *(The Message Bible)* "

Grief, pain, and sorrow can look different for everyone. These emotions are universal, touching everyone at some point in their life. Grief can cause various responses such as depression, anxiety, fear, loneliness, and even a sense of separation from God.

When most people think of grief, they consider the passing of a loved one. However, grief can stem from many losses: a job, a divorce or separation, a long friendship, a home through foreclosure, or even the loss of childhood due to trauma.

Your grief, and the way you are grieving, may look different from someone else's. But God's promise remains the same. He sees you, knows your pain, and desires to comfort you more now than ever before.

I want you to know today that whatever grief you are dealing with, you have not been forgotten.

Deuteronomy 31:8 (The Message Bible):

"God is striding ahead of you. He's right there with you. He won't let you down: He won't leave you. Don't be intimidated. Don't worry."

Christ feels and sees your pain. He rejoices when we rejoice, and He grieves when we grieve.

Many times, in our sorrow and grief, we believe God is far from us. We settle into our emotions and allow the enemy to torment us. The enemy might say, "See, God left you. You're all alone. Not even God loves you. If God is so good, why would He allow you to experience heartbreak?" These statements are far from the truth. They are tricks of the enemy designed to draw you away from God, instead of drawing you closer so you can feel His great comfort and restoration.

It Is In our times of sorrow and grief that God Is closer to us than at any other time. It is during these times that if we call out to Him, we can rest in His bosom and take comfort knowing He sees us, sees our pain, and is the Great Comforter. God does not make empty promises. If He said it, it will be so.

Hebrews 13:5 (The Message Bible):
"God assures us, 'I'll never let you down, never walk off and leave you.'"

No matter what your situation looks like today, no matter the tears you're crying, our Father is right there with you. He wants you to rest in His bosom. He wants to rock you in His arms and remind you that all is going to be okay.

He wants to let you know that you are never alone, and He is not going anywhere.

Because of His promises, when your tears have been wiped dry and this season of grief and mourning is over, you will be fully restored and have exceeding joy!

Prayer:

Father, I ask You to touch Your child reading this right now. Lord, let them feel Your presence all around them. Lord, hold them close in Your bosom and remind them that anytime we are going through sorrow or grief, You are closer to us than at any other time. Remind them that their suffering is not in silence, and You have not forgotten them. You are a Father who restores. You will restore their peace and their joy. And even out of this, they will see a miracle. Father, I ask that You give them peace that surpasses understanding and Your everlasting joy.

Father, You remind us in Ecclesiastes that there is a season for everything. This gives us hope that no matter what we are going through, it is temporary, and Your everlasting joy is a sweet, sweet promise. Thank You for Your promises, Lord. Thank You that if You did it once, You will do it again. Thank You that Your promises are always yes and Amen. Thank You that even when we feel You are far away, You are always close, watching over us, loving us, and wanting the best for us always. Thank You for the joy that comes in the morning. Thank You that if Your eyes are on the smallest of us, how much more are they on Your children. Father, thank You for restoration. Thank You for Your mighty healing power. Thank You for Your comfort when our hearts are broken. Thank You for protecting our minds so we stay focused on You and do not give in to the thoughts and snares of the enemy. Thank You, Father, for everything You have done and will do to fully restore, strengthen, and heal Your child. We love and praise You, our mighty Father. Amen.

ABOUT THE AUTHOR

Suelynn is a woman of God, deeply committed to seeking His heart. Her main purpose is to live according to His word, go wherever He leads, and always offer an unapologetic "Yes," regardless of the circumstances.

While preparing her chapter, God impressed upon her that she has experienced grief many times, yet He restored her and is now using those moments for His purpose. Suelynn was unexpectedly widowed at the age of 21, just three months after losing her father. She later endured the loss of her son's father as well. Through God's incredible restoration, she emerged from these experiences and now ministers to others who have suffered loss.

Suelynn is a proud mother of her son, Kyle Glass, and her daughter, Amanda Ellis. She is also honored to be a bonus mom to Mariah Hynes, and Maria, John, and Niko Robledo.

Her children, bonus children, and her beloved fur babies—Spoofy, Indigo, Squeaky, and Einstein—bring her the greatest joy.

Suelynn possesses the gifts of peace, joy, and encouragement, which she uses when praying with others, especially women who have lived through abusive situations. She dedicates her life to serving God and His people. One of her most frequently spoken sayings is, "The greatest death I could die is with my last breath, serving God and His sheep."

CHAPTER 28

REMOVE THE BAGGAGE TO BECOME FREE

La'Tonya McMahon Jenkins

Daily problems, situation and people will weigh you down and take your focus off of what God wants to do for you. God will tell you to leave it all, but you feel that you need all you have to stay alive. Once you ignore God instruction and follow you heart and it's desire, you will be empty without God and his word. Leave all that will weight you down—all that will cause you to get distracted that you will not do God's work and stop spreading his word. All you need is God and the strength to follow His word. All who don't accept you and the word of God, leave! Walk away and dust your feet off.

God will allow people you have not met to take you in and take care of you. God will supply all your needs. He wants us to place the personal issues and situations all at His feet and to trust and depend totally on Him. Trust God and His direction though His word. God wants us to forget all we know to listen more to His word, which will guide us to Him.

Let go and breathe so God can do the rest. All you can imagine will happen according to His Word. The load must be lightened to trust and experience His grace and mercy. Those who watch you will see God at work in your life. God's Word will never fail, and your life will bear evidence of it daily.

Prayer:

God, forgive us for all the times we have not followed or listened to You. Thank You for Your Word as we trust Your plan. Show us how to lay down our baggage full of our desires and plans. Show us how to move when You say move and speak Your Word only when You allow us to. Remind us to pack light, for all we need is You and Your Word to reach the plan You have for us. You are our Master, and we will follow Your plan as we learn to move in Your timing, not ours. In Jesus' name, Amen. Let go and Breathe so God can and will do the rest. All you can and will imagine will happen according to his word. The load has to be lightened to trust to experience his grace and mercy. All that will watch you will see God work in your life. God's word will never fell which your life will have all evidence in your daily life.

ABOUT THE AUTHOR

La'Tonya Contrail McMahon-Jenkins, born on January 30th in LaMarque, Texas, now resides in Humble, Texas. As the eldest of four siblings, she is a proud mother of two sons, two daughters, and a loving "Glam" to two beautiful granddaughters. La'Tonya grew up in Hitchcock, Texas, and graduated third in her class of 1986, earning recognition in the National Honor Society and being featured in *Who's Who Among High School Students*. She went on to study at Lamar University in Beaumont, Texas, and College of the Mainland in Texas City, Texas.

With over 30 years of experience in customer service, including a decade at NASA Space Center in Houston, La'Tonya has excelled in professional roles while also pursuing her entrepreneurial passions. Currently, she serves as an Independent Mary Kay Consultant in Humble, Texas.

Her creative talents emerged early on, with a gift for writing poetry and a passion for photography, which led her to establish Beyond the Lens Photography (BTL) ten years ago. BTL specializes in "Capturing stories that last a lifetime" and has been featured in *Overcomer* and *Voyage Houston* magazines. Her work includes capturing weddings, events, and serving as the official photographer for the Woman Arise Conferences in 2023 and 2024. She has also collaborated with Lady Silk Production, Tyler Governor Photography, and Sacrifice 4 Self.

Currently, La'Tonya is finishing her first year at a middle school in Humble. In her free time, she enjoys quality family time, traveling with her sister, hosting ladies' nights for her sisterhood sisters, and staying active at the gym. A devoted Woman of God, she attends The Point Christian Outreach Ministries in Houston and is an active member of Hope Renewal Global, passionately empowering women to reach their full potential.

La'Tonya is thrilled and blessed to be a part of the "He Restores My Soul" book collaboration, marking her debut as a first-time author. With a strong faith in God's timing and faithfulness, La'Tonya looks forward to continuing her journey as a writer, photographer, and advocate for women's empowerment.

CHAPTER 29

OUR SOULS ARE BEING REPAIRED, HALLELUJAH!

Fran Crawford

> 66
> "Then all the people who were at the gate and the elders said, "We are witnesses. May the Lord make the woman, who is coming into your house, like Rachel and Leah, who together built up the house of Israel. May you act worthily in Ephrathah and be renowned in Bethlehem, and may your house be like the house of Perez, whom Tamar bore to Judah, because of the offspring that the Lord will give you by this young woman.""
>
> **—Ruth 4:11-12** 99

God is sovereign, and in the darkest moments of your life, He will repair, refresh, and restore your soul.

In the book of Ruth, Naomi lost her husband and then her sons, becoming bitter with God and requesting to be called Mara:

"Don't call me Naomi," she told them. "Call me Mara, because the Almighty has made my life very bitter." (Ruth 1:20)

Naomi blamed God for her tragic losses and urged her daughters-in-law to leave her and continue their lives. However, Ruth decided to stay with Naomi and trust her God. Our strategic God had a plan to restore all that was lost for both women.

When you feel that all is lost, don't lean on your own understanding. In all your ways, acknowledge God, and He will direct your paths if you only listen and obey. Get into the posture of prayer, quiet your spirit, and wait for a response from the Father.

The women returned to Naomi's hometown, where Ruth met Boaz while working in the field. Boaz became her redeemer; they married, had a son, and this union produced the seed of our Savior Jesus Christ. Ruth's focus was providing for herself and Naomi, and our great God not only repaired her heart but also Naomi's. Souls were repaired, restored, revived, and reestablished because Ruth decided to follow God's plan. Let's follow Ruth's example and lay our wounded souls at the altar, allowing the Father to repair the intricate parts of our souls.

Prayer:

Father, in Jesus' name, we thank You for being Lord, healer, deliverer, sovereign, merciful, and kind in all Your ways. We repent for not trusting You with our hearts, situations, and lives. We make a conscious decision to rely on Your word, which states that we should cast our cares on You because You care for us.

We give You glory in advance for repairing the open and hidden parts of our souls. The healing oil is being applied to every area, which will catapult our bloodline. We know You have heard our prayers, and we expect that the God who is able, through His mighty power at work within us, will accomplish infinitely more than we might ask or think. Amen!

ABOUT THE AUTHOR

Francine "Fran" Crawford was born in Washington, DC and is the youngest of six siblings. She's the proud mom of 2 adult children and the GiGi of 11 grandchildren. She's been a member of Greater Mt. Calvary Holy Church for almost 30 years. Currently, she is a member of the Intercessory Prayer, Nurses Ministries, and the Alfred A. Owens Chorale. Works at the Department of Housing and Urban Development as a Marketing and Outreach Specialist. Her heartbeat has a non-profit, Employment Opportunities and Resource Center, Inc. which assist those with employment opportunities, training, provide resources for (healthcare, training, resume writing, clothing, food, housing).

Fran is an Intercessor and prays every Friday morning at 7am in a private group on Facebook, Strength for the grieving by the Grieving. She's a survivor of domestic violence and molestation and believes that you're never stuck in anything because God always make a way of escape. If you want to be free from anything, develop a consistent prayer life, seek wise counsel, and ask God for a circle of Intercessors.

One of her favorite scriptures is Galatians 5:1 (Easy) – Christ made us free so that we can be really free! So be strong and do not turn back. Do not let yourselves become slaves to the Jewish rules again.

If you would like to contact Fran her email address is francinecunningham@gmail.com.

CHAPTER 30

PRAYER IS NOT FOR QUITTERS

Minnie Meeks-Clayton

> " *"So I say to you, ask and keep on asking, and it will be given to you; seek and keep on seeking, and you will find; knock and keep on knocking, and the door will be opened to you. For everyone who [persistently] asks, receives; and he who [persistently] seeks, finds; and to him who [persistently] knocks, the door will be opened."*
> *–Luke 11:9-10* "

Have you ever felt like giving up on prayer because you didn't see immediate results? What if I told you that prayer is not for quitters but for those who persist? Today, let's explore the transformative power of persistent prayer and how it aligns our hearts with God's desires.

In Luke 11:9-10 (AMP), Jesus tells us, "So I say to you, ask and keep on asking, and it will be given to you; seek and keep on seeking, and you will find; knock and keep on knocking, and the door will be opened to you.

For everyone who [persistently] asks, receives; and he who [persistently] seeks, finds; and to him who [persistently] knocks, the door will be opened."

Prayer is not for quitters. It isn't a mere ritual where a genie pops out to grant every wish. Instead, it is a deeply intimate process that connects us with God. Through prayer, God invites us to align our desires with His, transforming us in the process.

God has established prayer as a conduit through which the power of heaven changes the circumstances of the earth. He deliberately designed prayer to draw us into His desires and transform our hearts until His desires become our own.

In Luke, Jesus instructs His disciples to keep on asking, seeking, and knocking—three areas of prayer that each require faith and perseverance.

Ask with Childlike Faith: Asking should be done with unpretentious faith, simple and trusting like a child asking a parent. As we ask, we should examine whether our petitions align with our inclinations or God's (Mark 11:24).

Seek with Determined Faith: Seeking goes beyond asking; it requires a determined faith that places us in a learning posture. Seeking involves being open and observant, actively looking for God's will and guidance in our lives (1 John 5:14).

Knock with Persistent Faith: Knocking implies a desire for access or entrance. It represents a persistent act of faith, where we keep knocking until we gain entry and come face to face with God. This form of prayer seeks the face of God rather than just His hand.

God does not require persistence in prayer because He needs to be worn down or convinced.

Instead, persistent prayer shapes us. It weans our hearts from desiring anything or anyone apart from God Himself. He promises that our persistence will be rewarded. Persistent prayer says, "I will look to God for my needs. I will continue to seek His supply and pray until God answers me. I don't pray until something happens; I pray until God answers."

Prayer:

Father, I pray for grace to pray consistently. Help me to pray without ceasing and not lose heart. I come against every spirit of weariness in the place of prayer. Grant me the power of consistency in my prayer life, in Jesus' name. Amen. Prayer is a journey that requires persistence, faith, and a willingness to align our hearts with God's. It is not about receiving immediate answers but about building a deep, trusting relationship with our Heavenly Father. Keep asking, keep seeking, and keep knocking, for in this persistent pursuit, we find God's peace, guidance, and provision.

This devotional reminds us that persistence in prayer is not about trying to convince God to act but about allowing Him to transform our hearts and align our desires with His. Keep asking, seeking, and knocking, for in doing so, you are drawn closer to God and His perfect will for your life.

ABOUT THE AUTHOR

Minnie Meeks-Clayton is a dedicated wife, mother, and accomplished professional. She has been married to her loving husband, David Clayton Jr., for 28 years and is the mother of two sons: David Clayton III and her late son, Caleb Clayton. Minnie has built a life filled with love, family, and purpose.

In addition to her role as a devoted mother, Minnie has pursued her educational and professional goals with determination. She holds two bachelor's degrees in accounting and business, as well as a master's degree in criminal justice. Her expertise has led to a successful 13-year career at Capital One, where she currently serves as an AML Sr Investigator I.

In 2021, Minnie founded Music Matters for Caleb, a non-profit organization in memory of her late son. Through this platform, she provides music education and scholarships to underprivileged children.

Minnie is also a successful entrepreneur, co-owning and operating two businesses: Smoke Me Happy BBQ, a popular barbecue food truck, and CJ's Creations, a creative design venture that showcases her artistic side.

Minnie is a true leader, philanthropist, and a devoted member of her community. Her inspiring story is a testament to the power of faith, hard work, and determination. She embodies her favorite Bible passage, Proverbs 3:5-6.

CHAPTER 31

PRESS IN ADVERSITY

Keseia Martin

> **"**
>
> *I will lift up mine eyes unto the hills, from which cometh my help. My help cometh from the Lord, which made heaven and earth.*
> **–Psalm 121:1-2 (KJV)**
>
> **"**

Press means to move or cause to move into a position of contact with something by exerting continuous physical force; apply pressure to.

Adversity: Difficulties; misfortune.

In the pressing, there is pruning, and in the pruning, there is preparation. The pressing and pruning don't feel good at all. Sometimes you feel so defeated and want to give up. But it is necessary to get to your destiny. Some seasons are lighter than others, but in all seasons, you have to learn to persevere. It is making you stronger and preparing you for greater things.

Have you ever thought about how wine is made? It looks and smells good, right? But it had to go through a process.

The process to make wine goes through six steps: Harvest, Crushing, Fermentation, Aging, Filtering.

- **Harvest:** The process or period of gathering crops. God already has the harvest prepared for you, but you have to pick the right grapes off the vine to produce the best wine.

- **Crushing:** This is the pressing part. As God presses and crushes us, He is molding and shaping us into His image and likeness.

- **Fermentation:** The chemical breakdown of a substance by bacteria, yeast, or other microorganisms. In this stage, God is still pruning you and making you new!

- **Aging:** The process of growing old. The wine tastes better once it sits for a while. It develops new flavors and aromas. Once you learn of God by reading and meditating on His Word and develop your prayer life, you will become seasoned in Christ. Your appearance will change, and your aroma will smell wonderful in God's nostrils! You won't look like what you've been through!

- **Filtering:** Passing through a device to remove unwanted material. In this stage, you're removing any and everything that's not of God. He's beginning to show you the people, places, and things that no longer need to be in your life.

Adversity comes to make you stronger. On the other side of adversity, there is victory! At times, it may seem like it's coming to take you out, but no weapon formed against you shall prosper. Just because your storm is present doesn't mean your God is absent. He is the author and finisher of your faith. Walk by faith and not by sight, trusting that God will do exactly what He said He's going to do.

He will never leave you or forsake you.

Psalm 121:1-2 says, "Look to the hills." Seek God for everything that you need. He will supply it for you. All of your help comes from the Father. I've learned on this faith walk that I can't make it in my own strength. God is the source of our strength. Continue to press toward the mark of the high calling of God in Christ Jesus (Philippians 3:14). Even in the midst of adversity, He sees you.

Prayer:

Father, I thank You for Your grace and mercy. I ask that You bless and keep me. I pray that You give me endurance and strength to continue to run the race. I ask that when I get weak, You will make me strong. Father, give me supernatural strength. Incline my ear to hear Your voice. Continue to lead, guide, and direct me into all truth. Lead me along the path of righteousness. Father, allow me to be unmovable and unshakable by any trial or tribulation that comes my way. Father, help me to press in adversity. In Jesus' name, Amen.

ABOUT THE AUTHOR

Keseia Martin is a dedicated mother to three wonderful children: Javari, 20; Yavonna, 18; and Aniyah, 12. She holds a degree in Healthcare from Ultimate Medical Academy and has accumulated 15 years of experience as a Personal Care Assistant in the healthcare field. Keseia has a deep passion for writing and enjoys vacationing with her family. She is also devoted to caring for the elderly. Keseia plans to return to school in the fall of 2024 to pursue a Nursing Degree. Her aspiration is to open her own hospice business, where she can continue to support and assist others as they transition to be with the Lord.

CHAPTER 32

HE RESTORES MY SOUL

Arshardae Perry

> 66 Now it happened as they went that He entered a certain village; and a certain woman named Martha welcomed Him into her house. And she had a sister called Mary, who also sat at Jesus' feet and heard His word. But Martha was distracted with much serving, and she approached Him and said, "Lord, do You not care that my sister has left me to serve alone? Therefore tell her to help me." And Jesus answered and said to her, "Martha, Martha, you are worried and troubled about many things. But one thing is needed, and Mary has chosen that good part, which shall not be taken away from her."
> --Luke 10:38-42 99

In the scriptures we see a description of Mary and Martha making two distinctive choices. Mary, as we know, chose the part that was needful, and it would not be taken from her. Martha chose to stick to the customary household hostess duties. I pray that as you read this you will begin to take a seat as Mary did and listen to what His heart says to you.

You're present with me, and you laugh with me?

The Lord says:

I will never leave you nor forsake you.

I am The True Friend.

I am with you in catastrophic events.

I like to hold your hand.

I enjoy your smile.

I'm faithful from generation to generation.

I've written your story.

I'm filling your capacity to trust me.

I'm right beside you.

I want you to desire me as I desire you.

I desire to be intimately involved.

I want to be your counsel, the one you whisper your questions to. The one you walk with at dusk.

I want to be the one that reveals true love to you.

I want to be the one you see when you look into the eyes of your spouse. I want to be the one you hear when his voice echoes through the corridors, resonating in the chambers of your heart.

I want to be the voice that acts like the defibrillator to jump start your heart, to jump start your life and cause you to see visions, and experience signs and wonders.

I am intimately affectionate toward you. You are my heart's desire and I love you!

I'm thinking of you always, hoping that you will remain with me. I know my love can be overwhelming & at times you'll feel a great need to flee, but I beg of you.

Remain!

Remain in Me and I will remain in you! In my presence you will experience many things, but one thing is certain I am Love.

I'm earnestly requesting that you rest and abide in My love for you.
This is how I want to Restore your soul.

Prayer:

Heavenly Father, perform your Word in me this day! I'm excited that you are in pursuit of me. Turn my heart to be in pursuit of you. Thank you for being my friend and being intimately affectionate towards me.

ABOUT THE AUTHOR

Arshardae was born to Valinda Webb and Benson Johnson on October of 1986. She graduated High School in 2005 and furthered her education at Northwestern State University. She obtained a BA in Social Work in May of 2009. She has taken great honor in loving people, learning from people, and leading people into their next.

Arshardae Perry loves Jesus Christ with all her heart, mind, and soul! She was raised in church to be a leader, to sing, dance, and to teach the gospel of Jesus Christ. She was born again and filled with the Holy Spirit September 9, 2001. Since then, her life pursuit has been to know Christ, the one, who apprehended her over a decade ago.

In 2013, Arshardae became a mother to a beautiful bouncing boy.

Shortly afterwards, she had the privilege to marry her husband, Earnest Perry in June of 2014. The grace of God allowed them to have two more children ages eight and one.

She is a published author in an anthology titled: Gracefully Broken and Heavenly Restored Vol II. Arshardae is excited about the plans God has for her and her family and looks forward to the great impact Hope Renewed Global is having in the earth.

CHAPTER 33

GOD RESTORES DAMAGED SOULS

Elder Carol Williams

> 66
>
> *"The LORD is my shepherd; I shall not want. He makes me to lie down in green pastures; He leads me beside the still waters. He restores my soul; He leads me in the paths of righteousness for His name's sake.*
> **-Psalm 23:1-3 (NKJV)**
>
> 99

Psalm 23 is a passage of scripture we often encounter that holds profound significance. While many focus on the Lord as their Shepherd, it's crucial to delve deeper into the concept of soul restoration. Yes, the Lord is your Shepherd and restores your soul. It's not just a restoration; it's a healing of your damaged soul—a process of immense importance in your spiritual journey.

Someone reading, your soul is damaged and requires urgent repair. Your soul is the appetite, mind, desire, emotion, and passion.

According to Dictionary.com, damage is defined as injury or harm that reduces value or usefulness. [3] Your appetite, mind, desire, emotion, and love are injured and have reduced the value of usefulness in the Kingdom. As you read this, I decree that your soul will no longer be damaged but healed to bring value and become useful in the Kingdom.

Before mentioning restoration in our text, I noticed the people lying down in green pastures and being led beside still waters. The Lord wants you to rest in a place of peace and tranquillity. He wants you to be still to give you clear vision and hearing of what's going on with your soul. Yes, settle yourself. You're too busy at the moment doing things that are damaging your soul. You're too busy doing things to avoid dealing with the real you. The enemy has deceived you into thinking it's everyone else with issues and problems. No, it's not everyone else. It's your damaged soul. Be still and know that the Lord wants to restore your damaged soul.

Accepting God's power to repair the damaged soul is essential. You've tried in your strength long enough. It's time to allow God's power to repair. Based on attempting to use your power to repair the soul, it looks impossible. It even looks impossible to me. However, with God, all things are possible. It doesn't matter how long your soul has been damaged, God can and will repair your damaged soul if you allow Him.

It's time to get active in repairing—get up and remove the grave clothes. The Lord desires your active participation in your restoration process, including changing what you see, hear, and speak about yourself.

---

[3] Dictionary.com | Meanings & Definitions of English Words. (2020). In Dictionary.com.
https://www.dictionary.com/browse/damage

How do you perceive yourself? Do you view yourself as valuable to the Kingdom? If others have told you that you're not valuable, will never amount to anything, or will always be damaged, it's easy to start believing those negative words and speaking them yourself. However, the Lord wants you to understand your true worth. He sees you as valuable and accepted. He wants you to view yourself as He sees you— significant and important. You are a kingdom builder!

Acceleration is on the horizon if you acknowledge your soul is damaged, accept God's power to repair it, and actively participate in your restoration. Yes, there's a quick redemption for the time loss of your damaged soul. The repair is happening quicker than you think. Yes, NOW until him that's able to do exceedingly abundantly above all that we ask or think, according to the power that worketh in you (Ephesians 3:20 KJV) [4]. With a repaired soul, you're about to accelerate and ascend to higher heights. There's no more blockage or hindrance to God's plans.

Prayer:

Father, thank You and we bless You for being God. There is no God greater than You. Thank You for taking the time to repair damaged souls. All praise belongs to You because what the devil meant for evil, You've turned around for their good. Yes, You have given them beauty for ashes. You have called them out of their grave, and now they're quickly accelerating and ascending to be who You've called them to be in the Kingdom with no limits or hesitation with a repaired soul.

---

[4] [Blue Letter Bible. (n.d.). Blue Letter Bible.
https://www.blueletterbible.org/

ABOUT THE AUTHOR

Elder Carol Williams, a woman of God, is called to minister the Word of God compassionately to those hurting, dealing with low self-esteem, and rejection. Through her impactful ministry, God has allowed her to share the message of hope in the U.S. and Uganda, bringing comfort and healing to countless individuals.

Elder Williams, founder of I Care Solutions, LLC. I Care Solutions is a community-based organization formed to improve the lives of grieving individuals, broken, outcasts, and disenfranchised. She's a registered nurse, an Advanced Grief Recovery Method Specialist, certified by the Grief Recovery Method Institute, and a former radio talk show host of the You Are Somebody Broadcast and The Mind Workout Radio Show. She formerly served as the director of an HIV/AIDS faith-based organization. Elder Carol is the author of several books, with her latest book entitled Moving and Being Productive in the Midst of Loss.

CHAPTER 34

DON'T PUT AWAY YOUR BASKET—YOUR HARVEST IS NOT OVER!

Michelle T Parran

When reflecting on the relationship between Ruth and Naomi, we often focus on Ruth's love and commitment to her mother-in-law, Naomi. However, it is equally important to consider Naomi, who felt there was no reason left to smile. She was overwhelmed with grief and shame after losing her husband and both sons in a land where they had sought refuge from famine. Naomi felt that her life had been reduced to nothing. She lamented, "I had everything when I left, but the Lord has brought me back with nothing. How can you still call me Naomi, when God has turned against me and made my life so hard?" (Ruth 1:21 CEV).

Perhaps you can relate to Naomi's despair. You might feel that certain aspects of your life have died or seem beyond repair, and you question how you can move forward. Yet, God has a plan that can transform your circumstances and change the trajectory of your life.

I once had two beautiful plants at church that others even mistook for artificial. However, due to overwatering and insufficient light, the leaves began to brown and new growth was spotty. I noticed small flying insects around the plants and was advised that my overwatering was the problem. Initially, I misunderstood and thought the dripping stems were like aloe or sap.

In an attempt to save them, I placed the plants outside to benefit from natural sunlight and rain, hoping they would recover. After a week, I considered replacing them, but then I noticed small signs of life—a tiny green shoot appeared where there seemed to be only dead matter. Soon after, a new leaf began to emerge from another pot.

Like Naomi, I thought the plants were beyond saving, but I didn't realize that growth was happening beneath the surface. Similarly, God works in our lives, nurturing our hearts and minds even when we cannot see the progress. We may mishandle our lives, but God is committed to removing excess and renewing our inner selves. In due season, we will emerge stronger, wiser, and better.

Ruth's perseverance and refusal to put away her basket led Naomi to reap a bountiful harvest, becoming the great-grandmother of King David. Naomi received a lasting blessing and is part of the lineage of Christ. So, don't give up. Your harvest is not over. There is still more waiting for you in the field.

Prayer:

Dear Heavenly Father, in the name of Jesus Christ, help me believe that You have a perfect plan for my life—a plan to prosper me and bring me success. Strengthen my faith that You can restore what seems dead. Allow Your Son to shine and Your Spirit to rain so that I may flourish and bear much fruit for Your Kingdom. In Jesus' name, Amen.

ABOUT THE AUTHOR

Pastor Michelle Parran is deeply committed to knowing God better and loving Him more, which led her to pursue a profound understanding of His Word. She contributes to this mission by serving on YouVersion's Content Review team. Pastor Michelle is a graduate of the Southern Difference Institute and the New Life Community School of Ministry & Bible Institute, where she earned a master's degree in religious studies.

Married to Pastor Robert E. Parran, Sr. for nearly 48 years, Michelle is a devoted wife, mother to two daughters and a bonus son, and a proud grandmother of six grandchildren and two great-granddaughters. She and her husband serve as associate pastors at The Master's Child Church, under the leadership of Bishop Melvin Robinson, Jr. Michelle is also an active member of Hope Renewed Global Ministries.

In the face of personal tragedy, including the loss of their son, Pastor Michelle boldly declared her unwavering commitment to "still serve God, praise God, and trust God." Despite the challenges posed by life changes and the pandemic, she continues to persevere in her faith and service.

CHAPTER 35

PROMISE KEEPER

Vanessa Eccles

> 66 *"When you pass through the waters, I will be with you; and through the rivers, they will not overwhelm you. When you walk through fire, you will not be scorched, nor will the flame burn you. Listen carefully, I am about to do a new thing; now it will spring forth; will you not be aware of it? I will even put a road in the wilderness, rivers in the desert."*
> **—Isaiah 43:2, 19** *(Amplified Bible)* 99

The Book of Isaiah is a prophecy about future events that would befall the people of Israel. Isaiah, a major prophet, revealed what God had shown him: the imminent captivity and exile to Babylon. Despite these forthcoming hardships and adversities, Isaiah offered encouragement with God's promise of deliverance.

Today's scripture reassures us of God's commitment and presence. He promised to be with the Israelites through the waters and the fire, a confirmation that, regardless of their circumstances, God would be present. They would not drown or burn; they were not alone and not without hope. God declared He would do something new, and He is not slack concerning His promise!

Sometimes, life's issues seem unbearable. You might face obstacles at work, health afflictions, financial disruptions, marital volatility, conflicts with your children, mental battles, weariness in your soul, dismay in your circumstances, or uncertainty in your next steps. It can push you to your breaking point, but you are not without hope! The same God who brought the Israelites out of Egypt and allowed them to cross the Red Sea on dry land, the same God who raised Job from his bed of affliction and gave him double for his trouble, the same God who protected Daniel from being devoured in the lions' den, the same God who shielded the three Hebrew boys in the fiery furnace, the same God who promised His presence in Isaiah, is the same God who is with you today!

Are you in a wilderness of stress and anxiety, in a desert of disappointment or grief? Do not fear or be dismayed. God will create a path of deliverance in your wilderness and provide places of restoration and healing in your desert. Psalm 23:1 & 3 reminds us that God is our shepherd who restores our souls. Additionally, Psalm 46:1 (Amplified Bible) declares, "God is our refuge and strength [mighty and impenetrable], a very present and well-proved help in trouble." If God said it, it is settled. He is a promise keeper!

Whatever issues or concerns you face, be confident in knowing the Lord is with you, and there is nothing too difficult for Him. Let Isaiah 41:10 (Amplified Bible) be a consistent reminder:

"Do not fear [anything], for I am with you; do not be afraid, for I am your God. I will strengthen you; be assured I will help you; I will certainly take hold of you with My righteous right hand [a hand of justice, of power, of victory, of salvation]."

Prayer:

Father, thank You for today's reminder that You are a promise keeper. Your love knows no bounds, and Your compassion never fails. You are faithful and the reason we have hope. Forgive us for not trusting Your word and the truth of Your commitment to our well-being. Step into the domain of our lives and do a new thing. We cast every care upon You because we know You care for us. Thank You for calming the storms and ordering our steps. Let the certainty of Your presence be with us today. You are God of all and never slack concerning Your promises. Amen.

ABOUT THE AUTHOR

Vanessa Eccles is an alumna of Howard University and currently works in accounting for a prominent law firm in Washington, D.C. She is married to Tyrrell Eccles, and together they have two sons, Christopher and Aden. Vanessa is an active member of The First Baptist Church of Glenarden International, where she contributes to the community through the Mission's Ministry.

In 2021, Vanessa was featured in the United Nations' International Women's Day article, "Women in Leadership: Achieving an Equal Future in a COVID-19 World." She embraces the belief that a merry heart is good like medicine and enjoys spending time with family and friends, laughing, reading, cooking, and baking. Vanessa deeply values the power of prayer and frequently reflects on Philippians 4:6-7 (KJV): "Be careful for nothing; but in every thing by prayer and supplication with thanksgiving let your requests be made known unto God.

And the peace of God, which passeth all understanding, shall keep your hearts and minds through Christ Jesus."

CHAPTER 36

BEAUTY FOR ASHES

Chasity Johnson

> **❝**
>
> *"To console those who mourn in Zion, To give them beauty for ashes, The oil of joy for mourning, The garment of praise for the spirit of heaviness; Theat they may be called trees of righteousness, The planting of the LORD, that He may be glorified."*
> **–Isaiah 61:3**
>
> **❞**

In Isaiah 6:13, this scripture reference is Isaiah's prophetic decree to the Jewish exiles that GOD would restore Jerusalem.GOD had sent him to proclaim the good news, free prisoners and comfort the brokenhearted. The road to restoration was not easy as they faced opposition along the way (Ezra 4; Nehemiah 4-5). Much faith was required to rebuild the temple and stand on the prophetic promise of GOD. Although you and I aren't returning from exile in Babylon, GOD knew we would experience some form of ostracism in our lives. During these times, He gave us the freedom to choose Him or sin.

Beauty for ashes represents GOD's redeeming power.There are many references of ashes in the bible.

In Ecclesiastes 3:20, it reads that "all go unto one place; all are of the dust, and all turn to dust again". In Job 2:8, the scripture says that Job repented in ashes. If you remember, Job was a righteous man who loved and honored GOD but he lost everything. He was stripped down to nothing and had to repent and have faith that GOD would restore everything that he lost. In 2 Peter 2:6, GOD reduced the cities of Sodom and Gomorrah to ashes as an example of what will happen to ungodly people.As you can see from these examples, ashes signify our human condition. Our ashes can be depression, fear, anxiety, abuse...and the list goes on.However, ashes remind us that trials produce humility and sacrifice brings renewal and restoration. Because of Jesus, we no longer have to sit in the ashes of our sins. He died for us so that we may be saved and have everlasting life (1 John 5:13).

Have you ever found yourself in a situation where everything going on around you looked like the opposite of what GOD promised you? ASHES. During these times, it is important to trust GOD. He knows that difficult times will arise but he offers us a crown of beauty, oil of gladness and invites us to put on the garment of praise in exchange for those ashes.When we decide to give GOD our whole selves, our view of life changes. Our circumstances may not change in that moment but the way we view them changes. GOD's word gives us hope. It is a beautiful reminder that He can take our worst circumstances and turn it into something great. BEAUTY. My question for you today is "What are your ashes?" GOD is encouraging us to trust him and not focus on our circumstances but focus on the promise.He is doing a new thing in us (Isaiah 43:18-19). Your breakthrough is coming! GOD WILL restore your soul.

Prayer:

Father,
You are there for us in those dark moments when we may not see a way out. You trade our grief for the oil of joy and gladness from your Spirit. You trade our despair for hope and praise. We choose to give you thanks today and every day because we know each season of darkness will fade away. You're greater than any trial or tribulation we face. Victory is ours because of Jesus Christ and we believe that we have a hope and a future. Your word says to seek you first and all good things will be added unto us. Thank you for trading our ashes for beauty. We praise you in Jesus' name. amen.

ABOUT THE AUTHOR

Chasity Johnson is a dedicated member of Victorious Life Christian Center, under the leadership of Apostle Latonia Moore. Through Apostle Moore's guidance, Chasity has learned to rely on her faith, prayer, and the pursuit of the life God intends for her. After experiencing losses and finding victory, she is committed to sharing her personal testimony of restoration with everyone she encounters.

Chasity is an accomplished military veteran, having served eight years in the United States Air Force. She holds credentials from COMPTIA and has earned a master's degree in Business Administration with a focus on Information Systems Management. Currently, she works as a Risk Management Specialist for the Department of Defense. A native of Pelham, GA, she now resides in San Antonio, TX. Outside of her career, Chasity is a devoted wife and mother who enjoys spending quality time with her family, trying new recipes, and reading inspirational books.

Made in the USA
Columbia, SC
22 October 2024

44794405R10091